D0855581

170
YEARS OF
SHOW
BUSINESS

170 YEARS OF SHOW BUSINESS

KATE MOSTEL *and* MADELINE GILFORD
with
JACK GILFORD *and* ZERO MOSTEL

Random House 🏠 New York

792.092
Mostel

Copyright © 1978 by Madeline Lee Gilford, Kazmos Productions, Inc., and Lucie Prinz
All rights reserved under International and Pan-American Copyright Conventions.
Published in the United States by Random House, Inc., New York, and simultaneously in
Canada by Random House of Canada Limited, Toronto.

Library of Congress Cataloging in Publication Data
Mostel, Kate Harkin.
170 years of show business.

1. Mostel, Kate Harkin. 2. Gilford,
Madeline Lee. 3. Gilford, Jack. 4. Mostel,
Zero, 1915–1977. 5. Actors—United States—
Biography. I. Gilford, Madeline Lee, joint
author. II. Title.
PN2285.M63   792'.028'0922[B]   77-90300
ISBN 0–394–41181–1

Manufactured in the United States of America
2 3 4 5 6 7 8 9
First Edition

Baker and Taylor

10⁰⁰

178

181 - 2517

But for whom . . .
Zero and Jack

★★

ACKNOWLEDGMENT

The authors wish to thank
Lucie Prinz
for all her grace and skill
in crocheting together the afghan
of our assorted lives.

To our editor, Charlotte Mayerson,
who looked at three handwritten chapters
from two backstage wives,
decided that they could become a book
and, through her perception and iron will,
made it happen.

Between us, Kate and Zero Mostel and Jack Gilford and I have logged about 170 years in that crazy world called show business. We've known each other for a long time. We've worked together, we've gone to lots of parties together, we've shared some of the good times and some of the very bad times. We've also done the usual things "normal" people do, like having babies and moving from one apartment to another. We've had arguments and we've made up. We've been very poor a lot of the time and then not so poor for a while. We've had lean years and a few fat ones. In short, we've shared so much that we've got about a million stories about ourselves and the fascinating, amusing and exasperating people we've known.

One day, one of us—I don't remember who—said for the umpteenth time, "Remember when . . .?" and I decided we should put all those stories together in one place, in a book. After a little while and a lot of persistence (the others would spell it differently), I got everyone to agree. It wasn't easy. Zero, for example, on hearing my idea, said, "That Madeline Gilford is a menace." He would growl and complain that Kate was wasting her time, but after he read the first pages, he declared himself "in." In fact, he made a little writing room for Kate in their house on Monhegan Island and went to the mainland to search out the perfect antique writing desk. Kate heard him say to the salesman about a lovely little desk, "No, no. That's too small. We need a serious desk. My wife's a writer."

So, Kate and I began to meet in the evenings while Jack and Zero were at the theater, after which we'd consult with the men around the edges—at night after performances, in the bathtub, over after-theater supper. Like women of an ancient tribe sitting around their campfires, telling the folk tales of their people, we'd spin an oral history of the Gilford-Mostel clan—and then fight with Zero and Jack (and between ourselves) to get the truly true facts.

We were having a great time, until we realized we'd have to write it all down. It came to us that we couldn't magically talk the book onto paper, and besides, we were interrupting each other so often that we'd end up with more footnotes and parentheses than text. Apparently, the four of us couldn't really write about the four of us together.

To simplify matters Kate was chosen as our spokesperson, our voice. From our contributions, Kate has fashioned, mostly in her words, our two-family, four-person chronicle, the collective history of the times of our lives.

What you've just read is the introduction to this book we had all agreed upon. Then, suddenly, with no warning, our circumstances changed.

On September 8, 1977, Zero Mostel died. For a long time none of us had the heart to think about much else—we certainly didn't have the courage to continue with our book, in which he plays such a major role.

But one day we all began to notice that a terrible noise was following us around. The uproar was terrific. It was Zero, of course

★★

INTRODUCTION

—Zero growling down at us. It was embarrassing because he was not a man who said things delicately. "What about that damn desk I just bought you? You're not using that desk!" he shouted.

Roaring, carrying on, right as usual, Zero got his way.

Madeline Gilford

October 1977

170
YEARS OF
SHOW
BUSINESS

1

★★★

At the opening of *A Funny Thing Happened on the Way to the Forum,* I wore a green print chiffon dress which had cost $230 and was designed by Ceil Chapman. It was the first designer dress this grown person, Kate Mostel, had ever bought in a real store. Usually, I got my designer clothes in Filene's basement whenever Zero worked near Boston. I sometimes think people go into show business just so they'll play Boston and get to shop at Filene's.

The chorus kids, called gypsies, had swell methods of getting bargains. They'd go to Filene's the first day they got to Boston and comb the racks for clothes from Neiman-Marcus, Bonwit's, Saks. The longer a dress stayed on the rack, the cheaper it got. If a girl wore a size 8 and found a real bargain, she'd go to the sizes 16–18 rack and hang her treasure amidst the ugly clothes for "large" women and hope that nobody would notice. That was part of the excitement—she was outsmarting someone. Every day during the run she'd check to see that the dress was still there, and then, on the last day she was in town, she'd go to the store and buy that perfect dress.

My luck wasn't so good. I once spent $30 on a Christian Dior N.Y. black peau de soie at Filene's, then spent $50 more trying to get it to look right. Dior had left off something critical, that essential "something" that would make it look like a dress. I tried gilets, scarves, flowers, collars and untold hours before the mirror until I finally threw in the towel and had a dressmaker cut it up the front to make a coat out of it.

But, for *Forum*, I was too elegant to shop at Loehmann's, Ohrbach's or Klein's, or any other New York "bargain" store. This time I was going first class, and it was Bonwit Teller that had the honor of dressing me for the opening night.

The first time I heard of *Forum* was around Christmas 1961, in a full-page announcement in the *Sunday Times*. Milton Berle was to star; the book was by Larry Gelbart and Bert Shevelove; the music and lyrics, by Steve Sondheim. It sounded like something I'd have to see.

Since I believe everything I read in the *Times*, I was astounded when Zero got a call from the Hal Prince office: George Abbott wanted to see him about starring in *Forum*. They sent the script to the house. (One way you can tell the difference between a star and a mere featured player is that a star gets the script delivered to him, while a featured player has to go pick it up.) Zero read it and then I read it. I loved it and Zero liked it, but from a distance. He agreed to go to Steve Sondheim's house to hear the score. (I don't know what billing you have to have to get Steve Sondheim to come to your house to play a score.)

Zero asked Steve what had happened to Milton Berle, and Steve said that Milton had wanted too many changes, that Mr. Abbott wanted to go with the show early in March and they liked the book with no changes.

I love musicals, and the thought of Zero starring in one was

5

****
170 YEARS OF SHOW BUSINESS

a childhood dream come true (only in my childhood dream *I* was the star). Zero had done *Rhinoceros* the year before and received a Tony award, the stage equivalent of an Oscar. He wasn't as anxious to go into another show as I was to have him do it, since he lacked my keen sense that you can't eat Tonys.

The next night at dinner with our kids, Josh and Toby, who were then fifteen and thirteen years old, I asked Zero what he was going to do. He said he didn't know, he wasn't sure, and added all the standard excuses actors give their wives in order not to take a job. My response was hysteria. All of the anxieties and doubts I'd had for the last several years poured out. I screamed, hollered and cried, and ended up with something like "If you don't take this part, I'll stab you. It's our first chance at security and you're blowing it."

What this was all about is that Zero was an intellectual snob and I'm a lowbrow ex-dancer from Philadelphia. (I'm probably the only person who went to London and was thrilled to be walking where Edgar Wallace once walked.) I loved *Forum*. It had all the craziness of the Marx Brothers' pictures and of London's "Crazy Gang." But Zero wouldn't commit himself. Instead, he sulked.

That Saturday night we were at a party with Jack and Madeline Gilford, and I complained to Jack that Zero had a good offer for a good part and he wasn't jumping at it. I told Jack that if Zero had been offered a play in Urdu, which only twenty people in New York would come to, he'd have jumped like Wilt Chamberlain. I asked Jack to talk to Zero and try to convince him to take the part. Either Jack was very persuasive or Zero was scared he'd be flank steak in the morning—but he signed.

A week or two later Jack called and said he'd been asked to audition for Hysterium, the foil for Zero and a wonderful part for Jack. Zero offered to read the part with him at the audition. They met at a rehearsal studio a couple of hours before the reading to warm up, and then Zero went to the theater with Jack.

Jack had worked with Mr. Abbott in *Drink to Me Only* and *Once upon a Mattress*. Zero had been in *Beggar's Holiday* fifteen years before, when Mr. Abbott was called in as play doctor in Boston. (That's the show where the director said, "Okay, let's go back to the original script, before the changes," and nobody had an original script. Nobody: not the author, John LaTouche, the composer, Duke Ellington, or the director, John Houseman.)

The audition Jack did with Zero obviously warmed some tired old hearts in the theater because Jack was signed. David Burns, John Carradine and Raymond Walburn were added to the cast, and it started to sound like fun and prosperity.

The office sent the score for Zero to learn, but he didn't happen to read music. Luckily, I play the piano just well enough so that I could teach him the songs (although Steve Sondheim writes with a lot of sharps and I hate sharps).

Rehearsals started with Mr. Abbott in charge, and I was in heaven. It was the first time in ten years that I was able to look into the future with optimism. I had had no idea that *Rhinoceros* would be so well received or that Zero would get almost a year's work out of it. That was Ionesco and not really commercial, and I hadn't dared hope for a run. But this looked so good—funny jokes, funny situations and funny people to play them. I don't aim too high. All I hoped was that *Forum* would run long enough for me to have the couch reupholstered. Beyond that I didn't dare think.

Madeline Gilford and I compared notes about rehearsals by phone (she knew a lot more than I did because Jack is a much better step-by-step reporter). During one of those calls Madeline told me that *she* hoped the show would run long enough to pay off their new station wagon.

At last it was time for the first run-through in New York with an audience, the day before the company was to leave for the opening in New Haven. Madeline and I sat together and laughed happily at every joke we knew and more happily at all the things we didn't know which had been added in four weeks of rehearsal. After the run-through, Judy Chaplin, who later married Hal Prince, came up the aisle and said, "Kate, reupholster everything."

On opening night in New Haven, Madeline and I again loved the show, the costumes, the wigs, the songs, the people, everything. It was, needless to say, a terrible blow to us when we read the reviews.

Most people have read about the troubles shows have out of town, and about Murphy's law (anything that can go wrong will go wrong), but this show had more troubles than most.

Steve Sondheim had never done both the music and lyrics for a show, although he had a great record with the lyrics for *West Side Story* and *Gypsy*. The music he'd written for *Forum* was fine for the book, and every song had a reason for being there, but there was no blockbuster of a melody in it. There was one nice ballad, "You're Lovely," and the rest was clever lyrics, sweet tunes—nothing to give you goose pimples.

The opening number, which David Burns sang, was a lighthearted, bouncy tune called "Love Is in the Air." Unfortunately, it didn't work as an opening, so we lost the song. In fact, we lost so many songs, there weren't enough left: no opening number, no solo for Jack, no finale.

To add to the difficulties, the wigs were awful, and the ingenue (who went on to become Karen Black) was replaced. The juvenile also got the ax, and infectious rewriting set in. There was so much rewritten that sometimes the authors got ahead of themselves. One night at "lunch," I asked Burt and Larry, "Listen, one thing bothers me—why is the virgin on the roof?" Larry said, "You'll know tomorrow." They had the punch line but hadn't figured out the build-up to it. Since it was a complicated plot, with love potions, passion potions and mistaken identities, it was possible for that to happen.

After a week and a half in New Haven, the show moved to Washington. We thought the reception would be better since the wigs had been scrapped, the two young people replaced and the plot juiced up. But no, Virginia, they didn't like it in Washington, either. *Forum* was a very risqué book for 1962. (I loved it when a kid at a matinée turned to his mother and asked in a low voice, "Mom, what's a eunuch?") Washington must have been shocked by the double entendres and sexy dances. This was before Elizabeth Ray and Fanne Fox.

Nevertheless, Burt and Larry kept rewriting, and the actors would play one version at rehearsal and another at night. Everybody got more and more tired: at one point, Larry sagged over the table in a restaurant and said, "I wish Hitler was alive and out of town with a musical."

One night after the show, Hal Prince came into Zero's dressing room. "Listen," he said, "we need help. We need some new songs, new staging, and an opening and closing number. Steve won't let anybody help but Jerry Robbins. Is that all right with you?" He asked Zero first because he was the star and also because he knew that Jerry had cooperated with HUAC (the House Un-American Activities Committee) and named Madeline Gilford, among others. Obviously, Robbins was not popular with blacklisted people like Jack and Zero and Madeline. *They* had been unfriendly witnesses in 1955.

I thought the decision about Robbins would be a tough one for Zero to make, but he immediately answered, "Listen, Hal, I'm a professional and Jerry's a professional, and if he can help the show, get him. Besides, we of the left do not blacklist." Isn't that a great exit line? Only, Zero didn't exit; Hal did, to phone Jerry to get down to Washington.

Zero called Jack into his dressing room and told him about Jerry Robbins. The idea of such an intimate working relationship with someone who had had such a devastating effect on all our lives was terrible for them. In fact, Jack immediately called Madeline in New York and said he would have to leave *Forum* because he couldn't possibly work with Jerry Robbins. Madeline insisted that he not blacklist himself, that the job was his. "Anyhow," she continued, "why should all of us who fought against McCarthyism be further penalized?" I can't remember whether Madeline began or ended this noble statement with "Don't be a schmuck—wouldn't you work for Warner Brothers?" (Warner Brothers had been the leaders in making the Hollywood blacklist total, and since Madeline had an uncle high up in the company's management, it hit close to home.)

The feeling between informers and the informed-upon ran very high. If I could have gotten away with it, I would have personally destroyed all of them by one of several extremely painful means: impalement on an umbrella or hot eggs under the armpits, for example. Actually, the practice at that time was to avoid being in a room with an informer, but if this was impossible, one simply didn't acknowledge the informer's presence.

Those meetings didn't happen often, though. The people who were blacklisted tended to associate mostly with each other— maybe because nobody else wanted them. Sometimes discussions at these soirees centered around how to treat an informer if accidentally you met one on the street. Zero, the suave model of a modern man of principle, met Lee J. Cobb on Central Park West many years after Lee had been a friendly witness. Lee approached Zero, put out his hand and said, "Hello, Zero." Zero drew back, shook his head violently, looked at the sidewalk and croaked, "No, no, no." But he kept it up for ten blocks. Not really the "chin up, stout fella" image, is it? Bob Gwathmey's down-home Virginia advice to us all was terse and wonderful: "Say how-do," he said, "and keep a-walkin'."

The day after Jerry Robbins joined the show in Washington, "George, Mr. Abbott, sir," as Zero referred to him, got the cast onstage and, without even introducing Robbins, said, "Jerry wants to show you how to do this scene," and Jerry took over. The strange thing is, the minute Zero and Jack were involved in the crucial struggle of a new show, the past faded instantly and "the show's the thing" won out.

In Washington, at Jerry's request, Steve Sondheim added the song "Comedy Tonight" for the opening, "I'm Calm" for Jack, and two more verses of "Everybody Ought to Have a Maid" for John Carradine and David Burns. Jerry staged a wild, wonderful chase involving Jack in a blond wig and white chiffon dress with Philia, the ingenue, and Domina, the character woman, outfitted in the same costume, going in and out of three doors, just missing each other each time. I can't explain what Robbins did, but there was a huge laugh every time the door opened and someone unexpected came out.

"Comedy Tonight" was sung by Zero as an actor presenting a company of players in a comedy for the enjoyment of the audience. When Zero said, "I now present the entire company," each actor entered alone from upstage center, came down to the footlights, formed a straight line and sang a whole chorus ending with "Tragedy tomorrow, comedy, comedy, comedy, comedy tonight."

After the applause, Zero said, "One, two, three," and the lights blacked out, the actors vanished and the play started—at exactly the point it had started in New Haven. We have yet to understand why the addition of that one number made a successful show out of almost the same material that people had not appreciated before. Maybe it's because the audience was told what was to come, that the show was a comedy. There were to be "cunning disguises, stunning surprises, nothing portentous or polite." They knew what they were expected to do . . . laugh! And so they did.

But there was still no finale, and the play continued to drift to a halt until Steve came up with a closing number two nights before the opening. Luckily, the members of the cast were quick studies who didn't chicken out easily, but even so it never played before an audience prior to opening night.

On that night we all sat at a table in New York's Forum of the Twelve Caesars (a restaurant which has since gone the way of the other Caesars). When the reviews came in, they were *raves*.

"I'm going to have the couch upholstered," I said to Zero.

"Go ahead," he said.

"And I'm going to get a mink coat," I said.

"Why?" he asked.

"Because I earned it," I told him.

I never let Zero forget that I made him take the job, just like he never let Jack forget that he auditioned with him. Each night in *Forum* when Zero stood nobly on the bench, potion cup in hand, pretending he was Socrates taking hemlock, he got a big laugh. During the laugh, without changing his heroic expression, he would manage to whisper to Jack standing below him, "Who got you this job?"

Forum was the first really big musical hit any of the four of us had ever had. It made Zero and Jack famous, and Madeline and I enjoyed the way the fame rubbed off on us—which happened only when we were with them, because who would recognize us unless they were there?

A lot of funny things happened to us on the way to *Forum*. Also some not-so-funny things. But the best way to tell a story, I guess, is to begin at the beginning. And I think I'll begin with me because it's the only time I'll get top billing.

2

★★

I, Kathryn Cecilia Harkin, was born in Philadelphia, the youngest child after seven boys. My mother was flabbergasted. She had no girls' clothing to hand down and didn't even
know how to make curls. Also, she had a boarding house to run and
she had to cook breakfast and dinner for sixteen people every day.
So, when people say, "As the only girl you must have been spoiled,"
I laugh a lot. I was so spoiled, they sent me to school when I was
three years old just to get me out of the house.

I think that's also why I went to dancing school four days a
week, to piano lessons twice a week and on Saturdays took elocution.
(Once my mother also threw in swimming lessons, but that only
lasted a season. At that time I learned so well and was so good at
the sport, I won a contest for the Australian crawl. The secret of my
championship was that I didn't go anywhere. While the others were
going up and down the pool, I just swam in front of the judges where
they couldn't miss my high style.)

Although no one in my family was in show business (my
father was a gravestone cutter), some of the boarders were. Each year
the house filled up with the members of Fred Waring's Pennsyl-

vanians Orchestra, who were in the first show I ever saw, *Hello, Yourself.* I was sent to the performance with a candy-box bow stuck on my head and fell madly in love with one of the chorus boys. And with The Theater.

The mother of one of the kids in my dancing class was putting together an act and asked my mother if I could be in it. Thus a kids' act called "Broadway Varieties" was my first professional engagement. In those days child actors were more visible than they are today. Movies like the Our Gang comedies were all the rage, and children like Jackie Coogan and Shirley Temple were stealing scenes from adults like Charlie Chaplin and Bojangles Robinson. Kids were also an economic commodity. Every mother saw show business as a way to get her child, and maybe the whole family, out of the poverty in which they lived. There were kids' acts on the stage, in the movies and on the radio. The most popular of the children's radio variety shows was *The Horn & Hardart Children's Hour.* It lasted for years and introduced many people into show business, including my friend Madeline Rosalind Lederman Lee Gilford.

"Broadway Varieties" had a cast of five little girls. In our opening number, little Mildred imitated Gilda Gray, I was Marilyn Miller, the Emmons twins (I've always maintained there were more twins in those days) did the Dolly sisters and Marie played Texas Guinan, the legendary night club owner who said, "Hello, suckers." Marie's mother was our business manager. She was also our escort, took us to lunch and dinner, and made us up for every show. In those days you put lipstick on with the kind of stick you use to push your cuticles back. That's how you got those cupid bows. And on your lashes you used beading, which was mascara heated up in a little pan, and put on each eyelash with a toothpick. It made your eyelashes very long and on the end you made a little bead. The consistency was better if you spit in it instead of using water. This is another beauty secret of the stars.

We worked Fridays, Saturdays and Sundays, doing four

shows a day at movie theaters around Philadelphia. (In-between shows, we stood in the wings and saw the movies. It was years before I knew that all movie actors, even the little boy who played in *Sonny Boy*, looked like a very tall, thin three-year-old.) As business manager, Marie's mother was no great shakes. She assured us we were the highest-paid kids in Philadelphia, but I remember getting only $15 for the weekend. Since I was only eight or nine at the time, I didn't have much to say about salary. I also didn't see much of what I got.

My mother had a neat racket at the time: In those days, when you test-drove a car before buying it, you really got to go somewhere. My mother would go to the automobile showroom, say she was interested in a car and take it out for a trial spin to Mauch Chunk, Pennsylvania, or Blackwood, New Jersey, or wherever I was playing that weekend. I never knew what car to look for when I came out the stage door. One week there'd be a Jordan; the next, a Franklin, or an Auburn. I know all the antique cars of that period.

Before my mother learned to drive, one of my brothers, Gene or Vic, would have to give up their Saturday nights to pick me up. They must have rebelled at some point because suddenly my mother started to drive. And I do mean suddenly. No driving school for her: she just got up at five o'clock on Sunday mornings, when the streets were deserted, and drove all over downtown Philadelphia. Along the way she hit elevated pillars, parked cars, streetcars—anything that was in the way. The big joke in our family was that she had hit everything but the *Titanic*.

Soon, by driving the wrong way on a one-way street, she discovered that insurance companies pay out money. The judge said that even though she was going the wrong way, the other car shouldn't have hit her. This began a big series of small accidents. My mother once got her arm caught in the door of an elevated train while she was getting out. To her great astonishment, she collected

$500. Well, to our family this was comparable to the discovery of gold in Alaska, and she began to fall down as often as possible. She fell down in buses, tripped getting on elevators and escalators. Trolley cars were particularly golden for her because they had such high steps.

It was like *The Perils of Pauline* set in Philadelphia. Every time we needed a few dollars, my mother went out and fell down. I remember once seeing her stand in the doorway of her bedroom rocking from side to side, banging her arms on the doorway. When I asked her why she was torturing herself, she explained that the insurance inspector was a day late and she wanted to keep the bruises fresh. Need I say she had a "Philadelphia lawyer" abetting her in these escapades? He fit the old vaudeville joke, "That lawyer is so successful, he has his own ambulance."

The earliest piece of advice my mother ever gave me was "Never get hit by a mail truck. You can't sue the government." But she sued just about everyone else. Once she sued when my brother was hurt in a high school football game. Neither he nor I can imagine whom she sued, but she did it. And she must have collected big, because my brother remembers that she gave him a cut of $10. We figure she must have collected close to $500 for his share to have been that lavish.

To my mother, nothing was incurable. Anything could be "fixed" if you only put your mind to it. I was such a dope that I always did what I was told, but when she made all of us change our shoes to the opposite feet as soon as we got in the house so we wouldn't wear our heels down on one side only, there were distinct rumblings from the male children—especially Vic and Gene, who were fifteen and sixteen at the time. Fortunately, something else captured her attention and she forgot about the "change the feet" rule. But she remained convinced to her last days that everything was correctible. Twenty years later she was bathing one of my sons and said, "Kate, every time you give him a bath, hold him up for a minute by his head. He's got a short neck." She kept a sharp eye on that neck whenever she saw him.

She did have one fear, though: that I'd be vain. Every time she saw me looking in a mirror, she'd say, "Don't do that. You'll get vain." Once, at dinner, a boarder said, "Kate looks just like her mother." And another, probably hoping for a second helping of tapioca, said, "She'll never be as pretty as her mother." I don't know if I am or not. I can't seem to look in the mirror long enough to find out. Even when I go to buy a dress, I look at myself sidewise.

In spite of her worry, my mother sent me out on modeling jobs with my brother Bussy. The father of one of Bussy's friends was a commercial photographer. He used to do ads for bread or milk, and Bussy would pose for him and get $5 or so. Bussy was very good at it because he sat still, the way a model should. The day they sent me along, I was supposed to sit in a chair with one leg out and look at my beautiful new shoes. Holding that pose was beyond my eight-year-old capabilities. At the end of the session, the artist said, "Please, I don't want this child in here again. Don't bring her back."

When I was much older, seventeen, someone came to my dance class one day and asked if anyone wanted to do some modeling. I volunteered because they were going to pay, but it was a different kind of modeling. For this job I had to go down to the Housewares Show and model in a shower to demonstrate a new kind of shower head. I wore a pink satin bathing suit, and every half-hour or so, to the accompaniment of *Tales of the Vienna Woods*, I'd take a shower. They gave me $50 a week for that. Easiest job I ever had.

My mother was about five feet, two inches tall, and she had beautiful brown hair, brown eyes, white skin and very red cheeks. Her figure naturally showed the eight pregnancies and the Lord-knows-how-many miscarriages she had. It's hard to be Mrs. America when you're pregnant every two years. Her mouth was thin, even in the picture I have of her at age nineteen. She explained to me that when she was eighteen she'd gone to a dentist because of a toothache and he pulled all her upper teeth. She was so upset that she insisted on an upper plate before she left the office. Those were the days when you could buy teeth on a pushcart. No fitting, x-rays or pampering, but I guess that explains her tight-lipped expression.

She was very sensitive about her lack of education. After the third grade, she had to leave school and stay home to take care of the younger children in her family. She could read, but she was ashamed of her handwriting. In all my life I never had a letter from her. She always got my father or one of my brothers to do her writing. She could sign her name, but more than that she wouldn't expose to the eyes of a stranger, or even me. The first absolutely perfect mark I got in school was in the fifth grade, when they were teaching us to write checks. I got an E-plus, the highest mark, which pleased me, but because my mother wouldn't do it, I'd been making out checks and deposit and withdrawal slips since I was about seven. My mother would give me $75, or whatever the receipts from the roomers totaled that week, and I'd walk seven long Philadelphia blocks to the bank with a little toy pocketbook to keep the money in. I always had to ask the bank for her balance because she kept the amount in her head, not risking that anyone might see her figures. Her guess was never off by more than a few dollars.

My mother was not a warm, demonstrative woman. The only times she was tender toward me or my brothers was when we were sick. Then she allowed herself to show her love for us. She really didn't like anything mushy. She sang all day long, but never Irish songs because she said they were all sad. Her taste ran to popular chauvinistic songs like "Wop, wop, wop,/I wonder why they call me wop./First it's dago, guinea, macaroni./Now it's wop, wop, wop." She was the oldest girl in a family of four boys and three girls, and her younger brothers always looked on her as a mother and stayed with her when they were in town.

Uncle Jim was a captain on an oil tanker for the Atlantic Refining Company. He was "the rich uncle," as are all sailors the first days they're in port. He'd bring us Spanish shawls, Dutch shoes, castanets and other exotic presents. When he first came into town, he'd go to the theater and to ball games, taking my mother and whatever kid was around—which is how I got to see two World Series games one year. Like all sailors, he also considered time ashore wasted if he wasn't drunk, so if you didn't get him early, he was just another drunk instead of my nice rich uncle.

Uncle Tom, on the other hand, let nothing interfere with his drinking. He devoted himself to it, and my mother frequently got calls from Atlantic City, where he lived, to come down and get him out of some gutter or hospital. My brother Bussy, who is eighteen months older than I am, remembers one Christmas morning when he was having breakfast in the dining room and I was on the floor playing with a toy. Uncle Tom came in drunk, tripped over something and fell on top of me. At which point my mother said to Daddy, "Good heavens, look at Bussy, he's white as a sheet." Not a word about me, flat as a pancake.

Daddy had a couple of good drinkers on his side of the family, too, whom I was terribly ashamed of. I used to hide when any of them showed up. Such a background may explain my aversion to drunks and also that I'm a teetotaler, as were my mother and father. Once, during prohibition, I found three bottles of whiskey hidden in a closet, and I poured all three of them down the toilet. I expected all hell to break loose, but I never told anyone and it was never mentioned. What do you suppose they thought happened to all that booze? That some boarder stole it and had a quiet bender in his room?

We had peculiar childhoods, my brothers and I. We never

had a room of our own but would sleep in any room that wasn't rented that night. Before we went to bed, we'd kiss my mother good night and then ask what room we should sleep in. We also had to get fully washed and dressed before we came downstairs to breakfast. When my middle brother, Vic, got married, he said, "I'm going to get a bathrobe and never get dressed for breakfast again." Little did we know that one day not only would Vic eat grandly in his robe but he'd also be the officer in charge of all the gold in Fort Knox.

My parents didn't seem to get along very well. I spotted this right away when they didn't speak to each other for a year. I remember one sunny day I was going on a picnic to Riverview Amusement Park where there were all sorts of rides and shows. My mother packed me the standard picnic lunch in our family—hard-boiled eggs and bologna sandwiches. (I didn't learn until years later that people take a bird and a bottle in a fancy straw hamper on picnics. I wasn't as sophisticated as Irwin Shaw's son, who had been brought up in Paris: when his nurse took him to a restaurant after his first day in kindergarten and asked him what he'd like to order, he said, "I'll have a dozen oysters and a glass of white wine.") My father was sitting on the front porch as I left for the amusement park. When I kissed him goodbye, he gave me a dollar and said, "Don't tell your mother." When I kissed my mother goodbye, she gave me a dollar and said, "Don't tell your father." I probably could have had a real racket going for me, but I didn't have the brains.

When I was ten, my theatrical career came to a screeching halt. "Broadway Varieties" had exhausted all the outlying towns in Pennsylvania and New Jersey and we had outgrown our costumes. Besides, Wall Street crashed. The backdrop was folded, and school, which I had always loved, became the most important part of my life.

That summer my father got sick with what was diagnosed as

consumption, the disease so many of his stonecutter friends were supposed to have died of. My mother, in addition to taking care of the boarders, now took care of him. He had weighed about 160 pounds before he got sick, but when he died, two years later, he weighed barely 90 pounds. My mother used to lift him out of bed to change his linen and we all would empty bedpans and sputum boxes, which we burned in the coal stove. My mother was impassive, as usual. The only time I saw her cry was when a boarder left, saying he was afraid to stay because TB was contagious. Ironically, the hospital was never able to find any TB bacillus in any of the tests they did. He (as well as his dead friends) probably really had silicosis from inhaling all that stone dust, but then it looked like TB to us.

He was a lovely man, my father. He knew all the words to the songs he would sing to me while I was sitting on his lap, yet when I sang them to other people they wouldn't recognize the tunes. The reason for this was that my father was tone-deaf. But he sang anyhow, because in our house everybody sang. We sang while we washed the dishes. We sang whenever we went anywhere in the car. There were no car radios then, so we invented song games—musical "Ghost," for instance. Bussy would start a song, and wherever he stopped the next player would have to start another song with that word and continue singing until he came to a word he thought would give the next player trouble. If the next player couldn't start his song, he'd become a "G," and on it went until someone was a "Ghost." Amusing? Well, you had to be there.

Since I only got 10¢ a day for lunch, it didn't take me long to eat, so to fill in the extra time I used to sing popular songs with my friends. In those days you could buy song sheets, four- or eight-page tabloids that gave all the lyrics of the popular songs. I think I learned more from the songs I sang in the school lunchroom with my friends than I did in the classrooms. "Mississippi," for instance. To this day, every time I have to spell it I have to sing it. And

Constantinople and Chattanooga, all those cities I use so frequently every day in my writing, I learned from songs.

When I was twelve, my vacation from show business was over and it was back to work. I guess I'd gone through the awkward stage by then. The gap in my teeth closed, my legs had caught up with the rest of my body and my mother felt it was time to take up where I had left off. And now we really needed the money. At Elks' conventions, Lit Brothers Department Store shows, wherever they needed dancers, Kathryn Harkin was there. Madeline has been after me all these years to teach her the sailor's number I learned in those days, where we started out rowing, sitting on the floor, and ended up sprinkling sand on the stage while doing a soft shoe. But if I reveal the technique, everyone will be doing it.

It was back to four shows a day on the weekends until just before I graduated from high school, when my dancing teacher, Catherine Littlefield, started a ballet company and I became a member. It was called—surprise!—the Littlefield Ballet. We danced in high school auditoriums and private and public colleges. Only, this time I got $8 a performance. You understand, of course, that this was Culture. We danced to Debussy, Ravel, Prokofiev, Chopin, all those fellows. To this day, when I hear Chopin's *Valse Brilliante*, my toes curl up in my shoes. The truth is, all Chopin makes my feet hurt.

After a year or two in small auditoriums with her little company of fourteen dancers, Catherine Littlefield lusted for fame. She enlarged the company to sixty and put on much more elaborate productions. We did the first full-length *Sleeping Beauty* ever performed in this country. The Curtis Music School Orchestra played for that one. We also performed big original American ballets like *Barn Dance*, with music by Gottschalk and John Powell. This was very avant-garde for those days because the composers were American, the setting was rural and the dancers were dressed in country clothes—blue jeans and peasant skirts. People then thought ballet had to be danced to classical music by girls in tutus and toeshoes. One of my favorite ballets from those days was to the American composer Herbert Kingsley's music. It was called *Terminal* and was set in Grand Central Station, with movie stars, divorcées, shoeshine boys and all the other characters you'd find in a big railroad terminal. And you've wrung it out of me: some of the dancers were in blackface.

Finally we had real recognition in the ballet world. We were invited to dance in Paris at the Exposition in 1936. Such excitement. No one in my family had been to Europe, except my sailor uncle. Hell, no one in the neighborhood had ever left Pennsylvania.

We were to be in Europe eight weeks, four in Paris at the Champs Elysées Theatre, four in London at the Hippodrome, and a week each in Brussels and Deauville. We were to sail on the *Île de France* from New York. But the boss's husband, who was the backer, wasn't rich enough to pay us a real salary. The offer was $10 a week plus room and board. I told my mother about this great trip that was offered to me, and she vetoed the whole proposal on the principle that $10 a week was slave labor and a rich backer should pay a decent wage. She absolutely put her foot down.

In my first show of rebellion in eighteen years, I gave a wail that could be heard in Wyoming and shrieked, "I'm going whether you like it or not!" A strong proponent of the "If you can't lick 'em, join 'em" school, she came, too.

I had looked forward to going to Paris because even in Philadelphia I knew that Paris was the capital of *haute cuisine.* I had had four years of French in high school, and although I had never tasted any French food, I could pronounce it. And that's as far as I got because our company never ate anything even approaching *haute.* Our hotel, Cinq Rue Debrusse, had just opened for the 1936 Exposition, and they were still practicing their cooking when we arrived.

23

****

170 YEARS OF SHOW BUSINESS

We were their guinea pigs. Unfortunately, at least while we were there, they never learned how to cook anything that even approached the edible.

Oh, we were sports about it. We tasted everything that was brought to us—we were good kids and we were hungry. But every meal was such a disaster that we ended up eating only the bread and mustard that were on the table. To this day, my idea of a grand lunch is peanut butter and jelly on white bread, so you realize I'm not hard to please, but even I couldn't eat what that hotel served.

The *coup de grâce* (don't you love how much of this is written in real French) was when we were presented with a little something that, under its blanket of white sauce, looked like the underside of one of those turtles they used to sell in the five-and-ten. We didn't even *try* that but allez-ed over to the Pam-Pam restaurant across the street and ordered hot dogs and milk shakes. We had to. Our costumes were falling off our skinny bodies.

Today, when I listen to our food-loving, high-living friends, the kind who talk about what they'll be eating this evening at Grand Verfours before they've even begun their lunch at Tour d'Argent, I think fondly of Pam-Pam, the "little place in Paris" that saved our lives.

After Europe, where we were held over in London for an extra week, we were asked to be the resident dance company for the Chicago Civic Opera season. We changed our name, just for this run, back from the Philadelphia Ballet to the Littlefield Ballet and off we went. My mother left instructions when she got back to Philadelphia (she'd driven to Chicago to find me a hotel room cheap, but she discovered that there were none cheaper than the one the business manager booked): Spend one dollar a day for food and one dollar for a room and "send the rest back home." Which I did. So did everyone else. We all were about eighteen years old, and besides, I had had my rebellion for the year.

It was a beautiful time. We got $30 a week and only had to

work fifteen hours a day. I loved being in the Opera. All that singing made me feel right at home, although the songs were a little more highbrow than what they'd been chez Harkin. I heard *Lakmé* and *Lucia di Lammermoor* with Lily Pons; *Aïda* with Beniamino Gigli; James Melton as Pinkerton in *Madama Butterfly;* and many more of the great singers of the day. Quite a change for a girl who was raised on "Wop, Wop, Wop." I was no longer standing in the wings of a movie theater looking at tall, thin images on a screen. I was standing in the wings of an opera house, surrounded by great music, or I was onstage dancing to the music of Verdi and Bizet. But not to Puccini: there were no ballets in the Puccini operas scheduled for that season. We got to throw rose petals, however, in *Turandot.* Eva Turner sang it beautifully, though only a few opera buffs still remember her.

When the season ended in Chicago, we returned to Philadelphia and to the Depression. I was eighteen years old, but my mother still had to give me carfare, 15¢ a day for mad money, and enough for lunch and dinner. I was feeling guilty about adding to her financial trouble, and I was also getting tired of the "have toeshoes, will travel" routine. Besides, the pay wasn't good enough nor the work really steady. At about that time, the company got a job in Chicago, and while we were there a few of us went to the biggest night club in town, Chez Paree. Mike Fritzel, the club's owner, came to our table, looked us over and said he had jobs for anyone who wanted to stay in Chicago. A light bulb lit up over my head, like in the comic strips, and I realized my big moment had come. I said, "Me," and the deal was made. Thirty-five dollars a week, three shows a night: eight o'clock, twelve and two-thirty. A new show every six weeks, for which we rehearsed four hours a day for three weeks. And one rule: no dates with the musicians. To this day I don't know what night club owners have against musicians, but the penalty for disobeying that rule is being fired on the spot.

****

Telling Catherine Littlefield I was leaving the company was very hard because I felt about Miss Littlefield like Judy Garland felt about the Wicked Witch of the West. I have a very big mouth, but only behind people's backs. To their faces I'm a card-carrying coward. Though I was terribly afraid of what she'd say, she turned out to be quite gracious. She merely looked at me with her iceberg-blue eyes, opened the door and slammed it after me.

It's funny, but when I left the Philadelphia Ballet to work in night clubs and collect a salary every week, I thought I was happy about it. No more of the grind of classes and rehearsals every day, sick or well, rain or shine. In night clubs there was no competition for roles and no jealousy because another dancer had been assigned a part you knew was made for you. There was also no challenge and no necessity to work hard, or to fight your body to make it fall into positions which are not humanly possible.

A ballet dancer is always aiming for perfection, for the one correct way to do everything. Your leg has to be exactly so high, you have to do two beats with your legs while you leap in the air, your knees must be absolutely straight and your heels flat on the floor—or your knees bent and your heels off the floor. And your head has to work, too.

Ballet dancers are the quickest, smartest people in the entertainment industry. Look how they got to be dancers. You take a class every day of a half-hour of barre work—pliés, stretches, quick beats with the feet and other warm-up exercises. Then, when you get in the center of the floor, the teacher combines different steps in new ways every day, shows the routine to the class once, and the class does it. All sorts of variations follow, to develop balance, extension, leaps . . . After that, the whole thing begins again, this time on point.

The smartest pupil is usually placed in the front line, so the slower dancers can keep an eye on her during the class, but everyone learns fast. This training accounts for the fact that while rehearsing

26

****

MOSTEL/GILFORD

for a musical on Broadway, the dancers can learn and discard ten numbers, while the principals—if they're not dancers—are learning one. Whatever salary dancers get, they're underpaid.

Why, you may ask, if I feel so strongly about ballet, did I give it up? I guess money was one reason, but, more important, I'm afraid I don't have the self-confidence and the drive you need to be successful in dance. Maybe that's because when I asked my mother after every performance how I did, she'd say, "Fine, but that Joan McCracken is dancing better all the time."

Deep down, however, I must have felt that I made the wrong choice, because I didn't see any ballet company perform for six years after I left. I saw *Fancy Free*, Jerry Robbins' first ballet, and didn't go again until Nureyev was in Paris at his first performance after he defected. I don't know what to call the problem, but to sit in an audience and watch dancers do what I used to be able to do—and can't do now—is more than I can bear. Make of that what you will, Dr. Freud.

I think the loneliest moment of my life was when the train pulled out of the Chicago station taking the Littlefield Ballet and everyone I knew away, leaving me alone.

On departure, one of the older girls gave me the advice that used to be given to all chorus girls: "Do a good show every night because Ziegfeld may be out front." That was a joke because Ziegfeld was long dead, but the other bit of advice to chorus girls was "Get under a good man and work up."

I didn't need that bit. I never even had a date in Chicago. There I was, almost friendless, with nothing to do except sit out front and watch Helen Morgan, the headliner, and Mary Raye and Naldi, the dance team. (To this day I can say I worked with Helen Morgan. And I do. Often.)

People are always ganging up on the "new kid," but I think

chorus girls are the worst. They're jealous of anyone younger, prettier, thinner, blonder or brunetter than they are, or anyone who can dance better. Although I wasn't any of the younger, prettier, etc., things, I could dance better and I suppose after my cultural life in the ballet I had a slumming attitude toward night clubs that showed around the edges. This made me not too popular. The only friend I had was another new girl who roomed with me at the Croyden, a lively show business hotel. If an acrobatic act lived on your floor, you had to dodge the backflips when you opened the door. Animal acts, chimps, dogs, anything was welcome at the Croyden. It was really very homey. If you cared for that kind of thing.

I didn't, really, and life didn't improve when my roommate was kidnapped by her boyfriend. He had pleaded with her to come home, sending flowers, jewelry and presents. Finally, he came to take her out to dinner, but instead he took her back to Kansas City. Alone again, I was now also paying for a double room. The chimps tried, but even they couldn't cheer me up.

Meanwhile, other members of the Littlefield Ballet company were saying, "If that ugly Kathryn Harkin can get a job that pays, why can't we?" Back in New York, they auditioned for Chester Hale, a popular choreographer who supplied lines of chorus girls to night clubs and theaters in the New York area. Some of the Littlefield girls got jobs dancing at Ben Marden's Riviera in Fort Lee, and since there was still a job open, one of my friends suggested me.

I handed in my notice at Chez Paree, waved goodbye to the chimps and left. When I got to New York, I went to Chester Hale's audition, and he had me stand in line with the other girls. Then he walked down the line like General Patton inspecting the troops. He got to me and said, "Bleach your hair." Now, I've never thought of myself as Lady Godiva or anything like that, but I had nice healthy brown hair and I'd never considered bleaching it. I wasn't a blonde. Blondes were dumb or gold diggers, and I was a ballet dancer with brown hair. Like Toumanava, Baronova or Danilova. But the boss said, "Bleach." He looked a lot like Erich Von Stroheim, and his manner suggested that he'd have my fingernails pulled out if I didn't run for the peroxide. So I bleached. I hated myself as a blonde. I had a brunette soul, and I always felt as if I were in a costume when my hair wasn't brown. It gave me a permanent scar, that encounter with Chester Hale. I'm still a blonde, all these numberless years later.

We got $40 a week, did the same three shows a night I'd gotten used to in Chicago, and only two numbers in each show were on point (that means on your toes and it's hard on a girl's feet). It was an easy life. We'd take the subway to 168th Street at six o'clock every night, then the bus across the George Washington Bridge to Fort Lee, where we were dropped off at the Riviera. Three shows later, at four in the morning, we'd take the bus back to Manhattan.

The Riviera had the glamour of every night club you've ever seen in the movies. It overlooked the Hudson and the Manhattan skyline shone in the distance. There was no air conditioning, so the roof rolled back, the windows rolled down, the dance floor lit up and revolved, and the two bands swung around on a movable bandstand without stopping the music when they switched for the shows. The band leaders were Ted Fiorito and Carmen Cavallaro. (And we still weren't allowed to have dates with musicians.) Joe E. Lewis was the headliner, and anyone who needs to remember his routines of that period should write to me. I heard them three times a night for five months, and I still have them down pat.

We worked hard, and it was so hot that we'd put ice on our faces between numbers to keep the make-up from dripping. There was a cafeteria in the basement where we got a discount on food between shows, and we also sat out front with the customers if we were asked. When that happened, we ate a lot (we were as hungry as we'd been in Paris) and thereby saved a few bucks. It was surprising how many laughs we had in that cell block, in spite of the infected corns, sprained ankles and all the other ailments that are the dancer's occupational hazards.

We did lots of lavish production numbers with fancy lighting and elaborate costumes. For our middle number, as an example, we wore red velvet gowns completely covered in front but bare in back, down to the end of our spines, and we carried white ostrich fans. One night, in this regalia, I knelt down at the edge of the stage and faced a table at which were seated Tommy Manville and a few of his friends. For you young folks who don't know the name, Tommy Manville was a millionaire who was always getting married for a short time, but only to blondes, and always leaving a handsome settlement. As I knelt in front of him with my white ostrich fan, I saw the man next to him look up at me, nudge Manville and say, "There's a blonde." I thought my future was made, but Manville inspected me, turned down the corners of his mouth, shook his head and said whatever asbestos heirs say in place of "Yech."

When cold weather came, the Riviera job ended and I answered an ad in the *News* theater column for a ballet dancer at a club called the International Casino at Forty-fourth Street and Broadway. The show was an extravaganza with ballet dancers, tap dancers and show girls. And Henny Youngman. Yes, that Henny Youngman.

I replaced Nora Kaye, who went on to become one of the most celebrated American dancers. She had been fired for having a drink with a customer while sitting out front. It was the same old night club world with one exception. We were not allowed to put on our own costumes but had to wait for the wardrobe mistresses to do it. Isn't that bizarre? Nineteen years of developing double-jointed elbows shot to hell.

And I didn't even have to ask. Dates with musicians were not allowed.

A couple of jobs later, I was back in Philadelphia. By this time I was twenty and felt that life was passing me by.

When I heard that someone was forming a line to go to Rio de Janeiro, I was ready. Imagine being on a boat for fourteen days with most of the time spent dodging the ship's doctor, who had evidently picked me for his target on this trip. I felt like those girls who were always running away from Harpo Marx. I zoomed up and down stairs like a mad antelope—it was good for the thighs.

We rehearsed on the boat and opened at the Casino Atlantic in Rio. It was a big improvement in working conditions: only two shows a night, the first one at nine o'clock. The pay was $40 and we had trouble spending that. We were rich. Amethysts, aquamarines, topazes, perfumes, riding boots and alligator bags made to order—$40 went forever.

We were also the toast of the town. Brazilian men thought American girls were gorgeous because we had light hair (I was still a blonde) and fair complexions and were a little crazy. In all the time we were in Rio we never met a woman. One day, just to prove our power, we said to our Brazilian boyfriends, all of whom had mustaches: "Too boring. Shave them off." And they did. We were so crazy with boredom that one day we all dyed our hair black. The owner of the Casino blew his top. We had to bleach it back the next week. He hadn't bought brunettes. They had enough brunettes of their own. You'd think I would have gone bald from all the bleach, but no, my hair flourished.

After nine months, we finally went home because we heard on the radio that America was at war. It was 1940, so you know it wasn't, but we left anyway. The sobbing, hysterics and broken hearts that left on that boat would have brought joy to Louis B. Mayer. We hated to leave, and I'd love to go back but I hear it's no longer 25¢ for steak and French fries.

On the trip back, instead of the doctor chasing me, it

was the head purser. I'm sure the men who work on boats have a lottery. They each pick a female and bet how long it will take to make her. Otherwise, why this sudden popularity? I was only irresistible on the high seas. Remember Tommy Manville? But the purser persevered, and on the last night he asked me to get up early to see the skyline of New York as we entered the bay. Worn down by his pleading, I agreed. I got up at five in the morning, dressed and met him on the deck. Then, though you won't believe this, as we leaned against the rail he started to sing, "Dear one, the world is waiting for the sunrise." He was serious and really wanted to marry me. He even offered me his grandmother's engagement ring. The problem was, I couldn't stand his singing or much else about him. I wanted to keep the ring and give him the gate, but the older girls wouldn't let me.

After Rio, life seemed very dull in Philadelphia, mostly because I had no place to go every day. Many years later my friend Stanley Prager was in *Pajama Game,* the biggest hit any of our friends had had until then. I called to ask him how he felt about being in a smash, and he said, "It's a place to get a carton of coffee and go every night." I know how he felt. You were needed. They couldn't do it without you and that was fine.

I needed to be needed, too, so I went back to New York and auditioned for the Rockettes. (Now let me clear up a point. The Rockettes were at Radio City Music Hall. Still are. The Roxyettes —phooey—were at the Roxy, which has been torn down.) A Rockette got $42 a week for the first six months, $45 a week for the second six months, and $50 after a year. It was the only steady job in show business for a dancer. There were no TV shows, you remember. Even hits like *Too Many Girls, Yokel Boy* or *Let's Face It* only ran a season. There was no air conditioning in theaters and they usually closed for the summer. So, if you needed to eat regularly and you were lucky, you got into the Music Hall.

It was, however, comparable to working in a herring factory.

When you were rehearsing a show, you came in at nine o'clock in the morning. (If you were late twice, you were fired.) You rehearsed until lunch at noon, dressed for the first show at one-thirty and rehearsed after the first show until four, time for the second show. You had dinner in the cafeteria or out if you had a date. Then the third show and then, relentlessly, the last, which finished about ten o'clock. You were on your own until nine o'clock the following morning. It was swell. And the costume changes! After I left the Rockettes, I swore I'd never again change my clothes more than once a day.

Talk about tired. We used to keep beach rolls in the dressing room and unroll them to sleep on after rehearsal and before each show. Anyone coming in would have thought the plague had struck. We kept O'Henrys and Hershey Bars in our locked drawers, and when the half-hour call came over the loudspeaker we'd stoke up on candy—except for one skinny girl who would take a shower. We swore she was washing her skin off.

The Rockettes always followed the animal act. We therefore learned to dance in horse dung, camel dung, seal's herrings and dog dirt. One Christmas season we were dressed as Christmas trees, with light switches in our bellybuttons. At the climax of the act, we'd all —in modern talk—turn on.

One day, as eighteen of us Christmas trees were coming out of each side of the stage, we were horrified to see, center stage, a little man with a broom sweeping up the leavings of the previous act, an elephant. He swept away, eyes to the floor, as the music played and three dozen tall girls moved inexorably in his direction. He swept and swept as we one-two-three'd our way toward him in a leggy pincer movement which threatened to crush him forever. At the last moment he gathered himself together and got off, somehow, but we were all hysterical with laughter. Maybe he was deaf.

My mother used to say, "You get used to hanging if you hang

long enough," but even she would never have been able to get used
to riding in an elevator with a camel. They slobber at shoulder height
and smell like nothing else in the world. Thank heaven the Christmas show played only once a year.

I was lucky, though, because the two longest-running pictures were there when I was: *Mrs. Miniver* (ten weeks) and *Random
Harvest* (eleven weeks). When a picture plays that long, the stage
show stays, too. You do the same routine, get a week's vacation from
Thursday until Thursday, and don't have to rehearse except the day
before you come back. Of course, you only get this vacation once
a month. You work seven days a week the other three weeks. But
if the picture is a bomb and plays for only one week, you have to
be back on Monday morning at nine for new routines, new costume
fittings, more Baby Ruths.

One Sunday, between the first and second shows, Pearl Harbor really *was* bombed. The war certainly changed the routines at
the Music Hall. Instead of Jerome Kern or Cole Porter extravagan-
zas, we did a lot of military numbers—for example, sailors on the
deck of a battleship which fired directly at the audience with lots of
smoke for the finale. We always wanted a march because you just
had to walk in a straight line and do various patterns with the stage
rising and lowering and the turntable turning. You didn't have to
dance or kick, but there is one hazard in a march: if you get separated
from your line—easy during pinwheels and boxes and crosses—you
have a hell of a time catching up. The stage is separated into three
sections parallel to the footlights, and each section is an elevator. Are
you following? During our number, after leaving a straight line at
the footlights, the end girls and every ninth girl about-faced and
marched upstage (to the back) and the three elevators started to rise,
each to a different height. The object was to end up in your parallel
lines at right angles to the footlights, where more crossing and
about-faces and formations were done of the four levels. At one

performance we grandly stepped out to get to the top of the stairs, smartly about-faced and found that one unfortunate girl had lost her line and was running back and forth across the stage trying to catch up. With the about-faces and to-the-rear marches we were doing, she never did get back in line. And that remains my one fond memory of the Music Hall.

3

★★

While I was at the Music Hall, my oldest and best friend from Philadelphia, Eleanor Stoer, and her new husband, David Davis, were in New York on their honeymoon and they invited me to join them at Cafe Society Uptown. The bill that night was Teddy Wilson, Hazel Scott and a hot young comic who had been getting a lot of publicity in the few months he had been working there. He had the improbable name of Zero Mostel.

In those days comics didn't wear funny clothes, they dressed like real people in dinner jackets, black bow ties and patent-leather shoes. But Zero had on a rumpled navy blue suit, red tie and huaraches. His hair was combed in the first upsweep for men, parted just over his left ear and brushed up and over to cover his bare dome. Later, when he began to lose the hair on that side, he combed it all straight up from the back of his neck. This left a little fringe of about one inch at the bottom to ad-lib with. Not only did he have to fight baldness, he had to fight gravity.

Zero has been variously described as a boneless shad, a balloon and a whale. He has even been compared to Mayor Fiorello

LaGuardia of New York, but the Mayor was called "The Little Flower" not only because that was the translation of his first name but because he was small. Zero was six feet tall. Kyle Chrichton described him in *Life* magazine at the beginning of his career this way: "He is not big in an obscene and senile way; he is not even youthfully fat; he seems merely to be something loosely in burlap. His face is not only mobile but it has a faint trace of beauty. He is moonfaced with lugubrious brown eyes which he can control with incredible precision, rolling them back into his head in opposite directions when he chooses." Zero also had the trick of rolling his arms in and out of the sleeves of his terribly baggy suit to express every emotion from fear to modesty to embarrassment. It made him look double-jointed, but he said he was only "relaxed."

That night at Cafe Society he had on his one good blue serge suit. Someone described it as looking like a tent. It certainly didn't look like any suit I'd ever seen before. It became something of a trademark, and later on, when the original garment had turned a kind of sleazy gray from constant wear, Z went to a tailor to get a new one. His friends were afraid he'd lose his marvelous rumpled look, but his new brown model looked exactly like the old one. "I got it figured out," said Zero. "They can't *make* a suit to fit me."

Once, recently, when someone remarked how little he had changed over the years, I said, "Geez, if you start off fat and bald, what the hell else can happen to you?"

Now, you remember that I'd been in a couple of night clubs myself. I'd worked with a lot of comics, and they were all cast in the same mold. They told horse race jokes, mother-in-law jokes, drunk jokes—and I had heard them all. So I was bowled over when Zero came on and did his first number, which was called "The Bird Lover," or "The Ornithologist." He played a nutty professor who gave a lecture called "Whither Birds—Or, What the Hell Are We Going to Do with Them?" The punch line was delivered with a mad, shy leer: "Birds mate, you know." It brought the house down. Then Zero became Mr. Faulkner, a shy public school teacher who had to give a sex lecture. He ended his act with the Isolationist Senator Phineas T. Pellagra ("They call me by my first disease"), who gave a speech about Pearl Harbor which concluded with the immortal words: "What the hell was Hawaii doing in the Pacific?"

I was hooked immediately. I had always been a culture vulture, and since I had only finished high school I had a big inferiority complex about people who had gone to college. (One day *N.Y. Times* critic Brooks Atkinson was scheduled to come backstage at the Music Hall. So I went to the library to get a copy of Nietzsche, which I displayed carelessly on my dressing table. He didn't even notice it.) And there was Zero using words like "fiduciary" and "canard" and "ornithologist." I didn't know what circles you had to move in to use that kind of language or hear it regularly, but I knew it wasn't the Music Hall.

Fortunately, my friend's husband was "El Mingle." He talked to everybody, and when Eleanor and I came back from the ladies' room he was having a drink at the bar with Zero. Somehow or other, Zero ended up walking me home. On the way he told me lots of lies, like his name was really Remo Faruggio and he was born in Italy. When we got to my house, he walked me up to the third floor, and we made a date for dinner the next night. Then I put him in the shower with his clothes on. I've tried, for the purposes of this memoir, to remember why I did that, but I can't. Zero never could remember, either. Maybe I thought it would make sure he didn't forget me overnight.

If that was the case, it didn't work. Zero didn't show up the next night at the Gloucester House, where we had arranged to meet. I was furious. No self-respecting $50-a-week dancer has dinner in a real restaurant if she's buying. It's tuna on rye, hold the mayo and a Coke from the drugstore. And a Baby Ruth candy bar for dessert.

38

****

MOSTEL/GILFORD

I was good and mad because that dinner cost me $5.

The next day, however, Eleanor and David went back to Cafe Society before returning to Philadelphia. Zero asked them the name of the girl shower-giver and then he called me and apologized for the memory lapse. The next night he really did take me to dinner. And he paid. In the words of Mr. Faulkner, "When you let a boy carry your books, that's the moment when it all begins."

Zero was only twenty-seven when I met him, but he was a man. All the other guys I went out with were boys, interested in sports, popular songs, me or other boys. Never once had a political discussion crossed their lips, except during presidential campaigns when, strangely enough, they were all Republicans.

I didn't know much, but I did know I wasn't a Republican. I was no stranger to political talk, because my father had been a die-hard, lifelong socialist. When my mother married him, she threw out a trunkful of the socialist paper, *The Call*. She also disposed of several letters from Tom Mooney, written in jail, which I would love to have read. (It wasn't that she didn't like socialism. She was just cleaning up.) As a baby, in my bureau drawer—there was never a crib—I learned one doesn't cross a picket line, unions are for the people, and never trust an employer. But I'd never talked politics with a man I went out with.

I thought Zero knew everything. Before I met him, I was very unsure of myself. I'd been in a lot of shows, had traveled to a lot of places, but if I didn't have the right dress with the matching shoes and pocketbook to wear to an opening-night party, I got very nervous and unhappy.

Zero said to me, "What the hell are you worried about? You're twenty-three years old and you're beautiful and it doesn't matter what you wear. Fuck 'em all."

I was floored. I had never heard anyone say "fuck" out loud before. The Rockettes were very bourgeois, and anyone who said that word in those days whispered it. At first I was too shocked for Zero's advice to take, but over the years I practiced and finally began to believe it. Unfortunately, by that time I was no longer twenty-three and not as beautiful, but I had a backlog of unreleased "Fuck 'em alls." (Actually, now that I think of it, I had heard the word once before. When I was sixteen and traveling with a line of girls touring vaudeville houses, the word did come up. One of the girls, no matter where we were and despite the ever-present taboo, would end up romancing the trombone player. It was so odd—*always* the trombone player. What's more, nobody else ever had a date, not in Pittsburgh, or Washington or Cleveland . . . or Cincinnati . . . The secret turned out to be that the music for the trombonist was marked, on the second number: "Seventh from the left fucks.")

I was so innocent, I'm not sure I understood what everybody was laughing about. It wasn't until I met Zero that I got sophisticated. He even used to claim he taught me to read. If Zero provided me with a feeling of security, it was mostly because he was so smart. It was nice to have someone around the house who could answer any questions you might have. Though I'm not sure now that Zero always gave the right answers, they were quick and I believed him.

But if he forgot the words to a song he had to ask me.

On that second date I finally got Zero's true history. Of course, we all know how he loved to invent stories, so a few of even these details may not be the whole truth, but does it matter? His name was not Remo Faruggio and he wasn't Italian. His real name was Samuel Joel Mostel and he was Jewish (I had sort of guessed that). When I remarked that his mother must have been crazy for "l's," he said it just translated like that. His name in Hebrew was Simcha Yoel Mostel.

The name Zero had been given to him by Ivan Black, Cafe

★★

Society's press agent, who hoped it would make people say, "Here's a man who's made something of nothing." Zero himself, who lied furiously to interviewers, especially if he was getting bored, used to say that Zero was a reflection of his standing in school, or his rank in the family, or the state of his bank account or any other silly thing he could think of. To me it was a brilliant choice as a stage name, for the simple reason that when you run your eye quickly down a page of print it's stopped by the letter "Z." Try it and see.

Zero was born in Brooklyn, and when he was a year old the family (six boys and two girls) moved to Moodus, Connecticut. Zero's father had been a winemaker in New York City, where he had the only sacramental wine license in town. If he'd played his cards right he would have made a bundle, but somehow he lost his license and there they were on a farm in Connecticut. Zero remembered that they had cows and lambs and chickens. But his mother wasn't happy. She didn't want her children growing up in the country because they would become ignoramuses, so, contrary to the classic dream of all immigrants to get out of the Lower East Side and into the "good life" in the country, the Mostels moved back to the Lower East Side to find culture and happiness.

Zero's father, whose acute business sense Z inherited, sold his farm to his sister, and today it's called Banner Lodge, a beautiful resort on 600 acres of lovely, expensive Connecticut countryside.

Zero went to Seward Park High School and, eventually, to City College in New York. After he graduated, he had a lot of meaningless and menial jobs in factories and once or twice as a longshoreman. Then he got on the WPA art project. At this time he considered himself a full-time painter. He lived in a cold-water studio on Twenty-eighth Street and painted hundreds of canvases. "With easel and thumb," he once said.

It seems impossible that anyone could have lived through those times and not have known that there was a WPA, but I managed it. I had heard jokes about men leaning on their shovels at government expense, but I never knew there was an art project which was a way of employing unemployed artists who were on relief. Z got something like $23.65 a week to teach art. He lectured at various museums, giving what were known as "chalk talks." He'd stand in front of a painting and talk about it. Except this was Zero talking, remember. So half the audience was rolling on the floor laughing while the teacher was doing a hilarious routine on the serious subject of ART. These chalk talks soon became famous, and Zero began to get calls from people who wanted him to entertain at union halls. Often they would promise him $5 and when he got there give him $3. This helped prepare him for the blacklist days, when he was booked to entertain at hotels in the Catskills for $500 and would get only $300 when he got there.

One day a radio director and producer named Hyman Brown saw Zero at a benefit for China Relief and got him an audition with Barney Josephson of Cafe Society. Barney gave him a tryout, and on February 16, 1942, Zero made his debut. He was an immediate hit.

Ivan Black, the only press agent Zero ever had, did a marvelous job for him. Of course, Zero was never one of those shy shrinking violets who dread being seen. He had always done crazy things. Now Ivan would call Leonard Lyons or Earl Wilson or the people at *Life* and tell them about Zero's latest antics.

Zero was a natural-born zany, and once he "shaved" Sam Jaffe at a table at Lindy's using the whipped cream from Sam's strawberry shortcake. And he had a way of buttering a slice of bread with large, expansive strokes of the knife; when the bread was covered, he'd just continue buttering his wrist and then his sleeve, all the way up to the shoulder.

Subways were one of his favorite showcases. On one occasion he boarded a train with a cane, pretending to be blind. But crazy blind. He walked down the aisle, his arms groping, idly slapping people in the face, and made his way to his target—a section where an old lady was standing while an able-bodied man sat comfortably. Finally, because he was so ostentatiously handicapped, the man gave up his seat to Zero, who made a big production of reading the *Times* with his fingers as if it were in Braille. Then, at the perfect moment, Z got up and, with a cavalier bow, gave the old lady his seat. At the next stop he grandly got off the train.

Even later, when he didn't need the publicity, Zero couldn't resist such antics. Once I was waiting for him on the dock on Monhegan Island in Maine. He was coming home from some job he had taken to earn the loot to keep the family up there. Going to meet the boat is one of the few excitements of the day on Monhegan, so the dock was, as usual, crowded with practically the entire population of the place. The boat pulled in and I saw that Zero was lashed to the mast, calling out over the water, "We had a mutiny and we lost!"

When he was awarded his honorary Doctor of Letters at Middlebury College, Zero transformed a solemn occasion into two completely crazy hours. The dean was a Latin scholar, and when he made his opening remarks he threw in a few Latin phrases. Zero, from his seat, interjected a few remarks of his own—in Latin. David Rockefeller was also honored that day, and his interest in insects as well as his collection of 50,000 rare specimens was mentioned. Zero, unasked, stood up and said, "I also have a collection of fifty thousand insects. Cockroaches." Then, while his own introduction was being read, he sat on the dean's lap. The students and even the faculty loved it. It's too bad no one thought to tape his acceptance speech, because it was in the grand old tradition of Professor Faulkner.

Zero had been at Cafe Society for about six months when I met him. He was already very well known, yet in fact this big-time, one-of-a-kind comedian was making $15 less than the unknown eighth-from-the-left Rockette was getting at the Music Hall.

★★

But suddenly, within a few months, he was making what for him was lots of money. Working two shifts, at Cafe Society up and downtown, doing six shows a night, he must have been taking home a good $200 a week. He appeared as a regular on a popular radio show called *The Chamber Music Society of Lower Basin Street* and then he made his Broadway debut in a show called *Keep 'Em Laughing. Variety* reported that the first-nighters "rose nobly and generously to the occasion as they witnessed another new star being born."

By the summer of 1942 we were beginning to see quite a lot of each other. Zero went out to Hollywood to make his first picture, *Du Barry Was a Lady,* starring Red Skelton and Gene Kelly, and later in 1942 I went to visit him. I had visions of being taken to the Brown Derby, to Ciro's, to all those glamorous Hollywood night clubs. And where did we go? To Hollywood's finest Jewish delicatessen. I wanted to see Clark Gable and Lana Turner. Instead, I got to see the same Jewish waiters I saw in New York.

Zero had a $3,000-a-week contract in Hollywood, but they didn't use him for any movies after *Du Barry.* Since he'd only done a few routines from his night club act and had no dramatic connection with anyone else in the film, I can understand their lack of enthusiasm. He came back to New York and Cafe Society, and that's where the draft found him.

They sent him to Camp Upton, and in the beginning he loved it. He called me that first weekend and said, "Kate, it's wonderful here. Everyone is here. Martin Gable, Alfred Ryder, everyone." Then about a week later "everyone" went on a weekend pass and left the new recruit, who had no pass, all by himself. He thought since he was there they'd all stay with him and keep him company.

Altogether, Z really had a rotten time in the army. He was shifted from camp to camp until, finally, he completed his basic training. He wanted to go into what they called Special Services to entertain the troops, but no matter how many times he applied he couldn't get in. Someone had branded him a "premature anti-Fascist" because he had done all those benefits for the unions and China Relief and the Russian War Relief. It looked like he was destined to remain in the infantry, but he developed an ulcer and after about half a year he was given a military discharge.

I had a little military career, too. I enlisted in the WAAC's, the Women's Army Auxiliary Corps. They gave me a few weeks' furlough to tidy up my affairs, and while I was home they changed their name to the Women's Army Corps (WACs). Because bureaucracy then, as now, ran the government, we all had to reenlist in the newly named outfit. By that time Zero was just about out of the army, and he told me to try and get out of the WAC's. When I went for my second physical (we had to do *everything* all over again), I pointed out to the doctor that I had chronic asthma. "Of course you do," said the doctor, finally looking up my nose. "Anyone can see that." And that is how I got my honorable discharge.

Sam Jaffe, the actor, was Zero's best friend in show business. There's a Sam Jaffe, the agent, but he isn't the one I mean. Our Sam Jaffe was best known as Gunga Din in a flick of the same name and for being the 900-year-old lama in *Lost Horizon.* Later, he got famous with another generation on television when he played Dr. Zorba in the long-running series *Ben Casey.* He has a halo of wild gray hair and a saintly, gentle quality that reeks of just plain goodness. He's a sort of Jewish Mahatma Gandhi with clothes.

Sam and Zero had met at a radio show for war bonds and immediately captivated each other. They both spoke Yiddish, were raised on the Lower East Side and had gone to City College. In Philadelphia we would have said they were "sticker-uppers" for the underdogs. Sam, I think, could have started a religion of his own because he has such a spiritual effect on people. He rarely raises his

****

voice, he's a vegetarian, and he doesn't drink or smoke. His only bad habit is an addiction to dried raspberries, which used to be sold in drugstores. Since they're hard to come by now (nobody is out on the street pushing something that costs 25¢ a quarter-pound; it's easier to get heroin in New York than dried raspberries), he's had to transfer his lust to strawberry shortcake at the Farmer's Market in Hollywood, where he lives these days.

Since Zero mentioned his name only about forty times a minute, naturally the day came when I was to meet him. I was scared to death. I was going to meet a movie star who lived in Greenwich Village. I pictured his apartment as a penthouse with floor-to-ceiling windows, deep couches upholstered in beige velvet and a butler bringing in lovely food. I went to Saks and spent $60 on a new dress for the occasion. Then, because it was red, I worried it might not appeal to such a saint.

After my last show at the Music Hall and between Zero's shows at the Cafe, he took me downtown. I think Zero was nervous for fear Sam wouldn't like me. I know I was terrified.

Sam's fancy apartment was one room on the third floor over a drugstore on Eighth Street. The marvelous food was tea in a glass and fruit, and the "butler" was Sophie and Annie, his two sisters. While we were there, Sophie plucked at Sam's hair with a silk stocking pulled over her hand. I don't know what magic was in that stocking, but he's still got that fabulous hair.

Sam was known for his hospitality. He invited everyone he met on the street to come to dinner, and most of them accepted. In their tiny, kitchenless apartment Annie would whip up fish for Sam, meat for everyone else, vegetables, dessert, fruit, cheese, everything anyone could want. It was all done on a one-burner hot plate with a metal contraption that fitted over the top to transform it into an oven. There was no refrigerator, just a metal box in the bathroom filled with a large cake of ice where the butter, milk and other perishables were kept. Sol Burry, an actor friend of Sam's, emerged from the bathroom one night saying, "My God, I pissed in the Frigidaire!"

But, as it turned out, the surroundings didn't matter. Zero had scared me by emphasizing Sam's angelic qualities, but Sam was as much interested in Rabelaisian humor as philosophy and he liked to laugh and tell jokes just like we did. The two of them together were great entertainment for me. They spoke in a mixture of Yiddish and English, and I guess it was right about then that this Irish girl from Philadelphia began to learn Yiddish. Everything is funnier in Yiddish, I discovered.

I had passed the first test, and since by that time Zero and I were thinking about getting married, he introduced me to Emily Paley. It's not enough that a fellow has a saint for a friend. After all, any man is entitled to one idiosyncrasy. But it was too much when out of his back pocket Zero pulled a female counterpart to Sam Jaffe. Her full name was Emily Strunsky Paley.

Emily was a member of a Russian intellectual family, daughter of Albert Strunsky, a beloved Greenwich Village character. Because he happened to own most of the studios around Washington Square, Mr. Strunsky was landlord to many of the artists and writers who flourished in the Village during the Twenties and Thirties. He was a special brand of landlord. He simply didn't trust anyone who paid the rent on time. Zero rented a studio from him when he was a painter, and one week Albert came to collect the rent. When Zero said he didn't have it, Albert said, "That's all right. You know that guy upstairs? I don't trust him. Every week he pays on time. He must be up to something."

Albert would wait joyfully for the excuses the tenants would improvise. If, as usual, the tenant didn't have the rent, Albert would warn him sternly, give him another week to get it, and if he still couldn't pay would say he'd have to move. Then he'd put him into another studio, which he also owned. This practice went on for so long and with such regularity that one day Emily sent out bills to every tenant who was in arrears. When her father learned of this, he got so angry that Emily had to go in person to bring back the bills *and* apologize for having sent them.

Naturally, everyone who came to town to live in the Village and become an artist, writer, songwriter or playwright wanted to live in an Albert Strunsky building, and most of them did. Eugene O'Neill, Thomas Wolfe, Groucho Marx, Buddy DaSylva, John Huston—they were all Albert's tenants. Most of them were also in love with Emily.

They loved her for her doll of a father, of course, but the fact that she was very beautiful may have had something to do with it. If you think I'm going to say that she had the disposition of a viper, you're wrong. She was an angel, still is. I wouldn't let our children's godmother be anything else. She has the Mostel godmother account.

Though all those famous and handsome guys were in love with Emily, she had the good sense to marry one of the smartest, nicest men I ever knew—though not the handsomest. He didn't have much hair, and he was a little shorter than Emily. Once, when I asked her how she knew enough to marry Lou, she told me that he and his family used to come up to the resort hotel her parents ran in the summer. "Lou's family always had such a good time together," she said. "They were always laughing. I just thought how nice it would be to be part of such a happy, laughing family." Lou wrote the lyrics for some early songs by George Gershwin, who said about Emily, "A warm day in June could take lessons from you."

Emily taught me a lot of things, like how to give a party: make the first drink very strong so everyone will loosen up, then serve the rest of the drinks much weaker. She taught me how to cook Jewish dishes like chopped liver, stuffed cabbage and pot roast with potato dumplings. At one time early in our marriage I said to Zero,

"You know, if the FBI is tapping your phone, they're getting a hell of a lot of good recipes." And I needed recipes. My mother had sent me out into the world with a set of perfectly good directions for making such wholesome, goyish dishes as corned beef and cabbage, Philadelphia scrapple and creamed beef on toast—none of which Zero would eat.

The recipes didn't come from Emily herself. They were the property of her mother, Mascha, who lived with her. Mascha was the Russian Julia Child. At one memorable meal she made a salt-free dinner for Lou; a vegetarian meal for Sam Jaffe; and for Zero she went all out and gave him salt and meat and everything else he could want. As usual, I was on a diet and so got broiled chops with no sauces or butter.

In the summer of 1944 Emily and Lou rented a house in Long Branch, New Jersey, and Sam, Mascha, Lou and Em decided Zero and I should get married there. Sam had it all thought out: I would stay in New Jersey for the week, get the marriage license and have my blood test. Zero would have his in New York, and the next Friday night he and Sam and Tully Flaumenhauft (who was involved partly because he was Zero's friend and partly because he had a car) would drive to Long Branch. We would be married Sunday morning in the office of the mayor of Long Branch.

So, as always, I did as I was told. I got the license, booked the mayor and spent the week on the beach to get a little tan that might take attention away from my dress. It wasn't easy to locate the ugliest dress in New York, but with a sense of purpose and stick-to-it-iveness I had tracked it down. There was plenty of time to have the hem taken up (a little too much) and the bosom let out (a little too little), and thank God my face was red because the color of the dress was the definition of bilious green. It was eyelet cotton, too, although we didn't need the eyelet—we had enough ugliness without it. Was it just me or does everyone pick out the world's worst dress to get married in?

Emily, Mascha and I did all the necessary prenuptial things like shopping, cleaning and going to the beach. Then, on Friday night, Emily kept me company on the porch, rocking and waiting for Prince Charming and his entourage. At about eleven-thirty Emily got tired of rocking and went to bed, leaving me alone to sing under my breath, "There was I, waiting at the church."

He finally arrived, the Prince, around midnight. I found out later that Tully had held them up for some time while he tried to talk Zero out of the marriage. For one thing, he said Z should demand that I convert to Judaism before we got married. Zero resisted, and on July 2, 1944, we did get married in a simple but dignified ceremony spoiled only slightly by Sam, who carried on a running commentary in Yiddish and kicked Zero just as he was about to say, "I do," and by the fact that Zero forgot the ring. We had to borrow Emily's, but she hadn't had it off in twenty-five years and there was a lot of tugging and twisting until finally she went and put soap on it to make it slide off. The mayor had only allotted us fifteen minutes, and with these complications we exceeded the time limit a bit. When it was all over, I was an honest woman at last.

We went to Emily's for a wedding breakfast of bagels, Nova Scotia lox, cream cheese, sturgeon, whitefish, herring, and chopped liver—none of which I like. I longed for good old waffles and sausages. In my hideous green dress, and my sunburn, a little nauseated by this exotic buffet, I must have been the most uncomfortable bride since Frankenstein's. After we did the dishes, Zero, Tully and Lou went off to play golf. Emily took a nap. I don't remember where Sam was. I wound up on the beach as alone as I had been all week, only this time I was wearing a borrowed wedding ring.

To say that Zero didn't make a big announcement about our getting married is to put it mildly. In fact, he didn't tell anyone. Not long after we got back to New York we were sitting in Toots Shor's with Frank Loesser and his wife, and Frank, noticing my wedding ring (we did eventually get one of our own), asked Zero, "Did you finally get married?" Zero said no.

But he did tell Phil Loeb. And Phil was gracious and charming as always. "May I have the option on your first infidelity?" he asked.

Zero introduced me to Phil shortly after I met Sam Jaffe. I'd seen Phil in *The Band Wagon,* a revue which was the second show I ever saw in Philadelphia. I also saw him in *Sing Out the News* and, on the screen, in *Room Service* with the Marx Brothers and *Over 21* with Ruth Gordon. So I wasn't reverent about meeting him. I mean, I knew he wasn't a saint. I'd seen him in real life and could tell he had human qualities.

Phil's passion was Actors Equity, the union of theater actors. He was on the governing body for many years, and even if he was in a show on the road he'd fly in for the Tuesday afternoon meetings.

Phil had the unique ability of falling asleep at any time. In the middle of a crowded room, at a dinner party, anywhere. If he felt sleepy, he slept. Strangers seeing it for the first time were enthralled. And then we'd show them how, if you really needed him, you could wake him up. We'd be having a normal conversation and Phil would put his head down on whatever was near (once it was the corner of a grand piano keyboard) and start to snore. Someone would whisper, through the whole roomful of chatter, the two magic words "Actors Equity," and Phil would sit upright, wide awake, and say "What about Actors Equity?" It never failed. (I have a dog now with a similar trait. If I say, in a loud voice, "Who farted?" Max will slink from wherever he is to hide under the couch. It's all from Pavlov.)

We were Phil's guests on opening night when he appeared in a play called *Common Ground.* As the second act began, all of us were on the edge of our seats—and not because the plot was so suspenseful. Phil had told us that in the second act he had no lines at all. He just had to sit onstage and listen to a twenty-minute monologue by Luther Adler, the star of the show. Sure enough, when the curtain rose, there was Phil seated on the steps of the set, looking very relaxed. Too relaxed. Knowing his talent for a quick snooze, we were terrified. For the first five minutes we kept one eye on Luther and one eye on Phil, and after that we looked only at Phil. We were willing him awake, but soon he was breathing deeply. Dear God, I prayed, if you must let him sleep, at least see that he doesn't snore. He did, most certainly, go to sleep on that stage, and Zero and I exhausted ourselves trying to keep him from falling off the steps just by the sheer force of our eyes pinning his body to them. Fortunately, Luther's speech was a great tour de force, and the audience responded with such a thunder of applause that even Phil woke up. That night, somebody up there liked us.

Of course, I knew that Zero had been a painter before he went into show business. I knew that he had a studio on Twenty-eighth Street where he still painted every day. But I didn't realize that this would go on after we were married. I grew up reading *Hearst's International Cosmopolitan.* (When I was young, reading fast, I thought it was *Heart's Eternal Cosmopolitan.*) All the stories were love stories in which when people got married they did nice things together. They went to museums and movies, or they just strolled around New York hand in hand, chatting intimately and occasionally greeting friends. It was *très gentile* (that's French, pronounced "genteel"—not English, which in my crowd is pronounced "shiksa" and refers mainly to me).

I had looked forward to that. But Zero hadn't been reading the same stories. He'd read books in which a man gets married and keeps right on doing what he wants, with the little woman fending for herself.

The first day we got back from tying the knot, he was off to Twenty-eighth Street.

"Hey," I said, "we're married. Aren't you going to spend more time with me today?"

"Nope," he said, "I've got to paint," and he was gone.

I guess I thought marriage would make a difference and that saying "I do" would change Zero into an accountant or something. I thought that little ceremony had granted me power over Zero— which it turned out I didn't have.

What was so great about Twenty-eighth Street? Well, for one thing there was his studio. And then there were his old buddies: Herbie Kallem, the sculptor who had shared the studio with him since WPA days, and Henry Kallem, his brother, a painter who had a studio upstairs. And Henry Rothman, who didn't paint. He took photos and did framing and talked. Framed and talked and talked and talked. To this day, he frames and talks. You know who else was on Twenty-eighth Street? Remo Faruggio, famous from my first date with Zero. And Joe di Martini and Nick Luisi and a few others I still haven't met.

Those Twenty-eighth Street guys became our extended family, even though that term hadn't been invented in those days. They certainly influenced our lives in many ways. They stole Zero away from his bride and they got us to go to Monhegan, one of the most beautiful places on earth.

Monhegan is an island off the coast of Maine. It has always been a home for fishermen and lobstermen, and since the turn of the century for artists like Robert Henri, George Bellows and Rockwell Kent, who have spent their summers there. Over the years one artist brought another. One year Joe di Martini brought Herbie and the next year Herbie brought us and we've been going back every year since 1949.

Cleveland Amory in *The Last Resorts* explains how resorts develop. First the artists find a nice cheap beautiful place like Woodstock, Provincetown or Amagansett. Then the middle class comes in because it's cheap and beautiful. Finally rich people—the spoilers —hear about the place and buy up all the available land and property. Pretty soon it's too expensive for the artists. They have to move on and find another beautiful cheap place to summer in.

Monhegan is different. It stopped permanently at the middle-class stage because there's no more land to buy (it's a tiny island, seven-eighths of a mile wide by one mile long) and there are no houses to buy and there's no more building allowed because the water is limited. So we were lucky.

Zero was essentially a city person who hated the country. What he loved was good gray concrete. Perhaps this was because he was one of those people adored by mosquitoes. All he had to do was sit outside and for sixty miles around the word would go out to anything that flew and bit, "Hey, fellows, Zero's here." But in Monhegan there was so much wind that the mosquitoes were blown off course before they could find their juicy target. So Zero didn't really consider Monhegan the country and he loved it.

Also he had a studio there. Every morning he would disappear into it, emerge for the mail, go back and paint and not be seen again until five in the afternoon.

A lot of people have said that Zero really wanted to be thought of as a painter who happened to act now and then, that he was really happier painting than acting. I guess the truth is he was as happy painting as acting, not happier. I mean, he didn't feel terrible if he had nothing better to do than go into the studio.

He loved painting, but that doesn't mean he hated acting. After all, he could get up on a stage and have a huge theater full of people in tears or in stitches while he carried on as a Jewish milkman or a Roman slave or turned himself into a rampaging rhinoceros. Then there was all that applause. You'd have to be stupid not to like the applause or to enjoy being the highest-paid actor on Broadway.

Still, painting was very special to Zero. During the blacklist, when he couldn't work, it gave him an important creative outlet and someplace to go. He didn't have to lie around the house moaning. He was just as happy on Twenty-eighth Street as he would have been on Broadway.

Sometimes, but rarely, Zero talked about his painting. While he was in *Ulysses in Nighttown* on Broadway, our friend Jerry Tallmer interviewed him for the *New York Post* and asked if he was still going down to the studio during the run of that very demanding play. Zero said, "What else would I do?" and went on, "You know, when you're painting, your hand finds the color instinctively. Well, on Tuesday I took one stroke, wrong color, oh hell, I had ruined it. But the fact that you're *there*, in the studio, is marvelous."

Zero loved to teach about art, and he adored taking people to museums. Once he took me to a museum and we wandered around the galleries for hours. Every time he stood in front of a painting he'd say, "That's the greatest artist. That Picasso. He's the greatest." Whatever he stood in front of, that was the greatest. Finally I said to him, "Zero, get me out of here. I'm getting painting poisoning."

Feeling as he did about fascist Spain, Zero really had to fight with himself to go there. He decided to go when he realized that Franco could see all the paintings in the Prado that Zero wouldn't get to see unless he went. He especially wanted to see Hieronymus Bosch's *Garden of Earthly Delights*. He visited the museum and spent 100 hours just looking at it. And, as he told Tallmer in his interview, "On the last day I saw something in it I hadn't noticed before, an ass bent over with a pot of flowers on it."

In Spain during the shooting of *Forum* Jack and Zero went to the Prado every Sunday, their day off. Zero would select one room and explain, point out, tell the history of and talk about the artist of each painting in the room. If you've been there, you know each gallery in the Prado can take an entire day. Once Zero told Jack about the little church, out in the country, where Goya was buried. Jack went to see the grave, and when he came back he told Zero about being there. Zero had also made the trip. He'd gone all alone and had placed a bouquet of flowers on the great master's grave.

Zero's painting was very important to him, and it got to be important to me, too. In those early postnuptial days I felt about his leaving me go to Twenty-eighth Street the way some women feel about their husbands playing golf. But I got to accept the painting the way I got to accept Zero carrying on in restaurants. Like a friend once said, "If I wanted someone who behaved like an accountant, I should have married an accountant."

4

★★★

That's where Z and I were in 1943. Now, to get the act together, let's get the rest of the cast onstage.

While I was growing up with one foot in show business in Philadelphia, Madeline Lederman was leading a remarkably similar life over in the Bronx, Jewish–New York style. Madeline was the youngest of four children, three sisters and one brother. Her mother had come to New York as a teenager after crossing from Poland to Germany hidden in a hay wagon with her younger brother. She used to tell Madeline the hair-raising story of how the Cossacks drove their sabers through the hay and right by her nose. In fact, each year that she told the story, the sword came closer.

Madeline's maternal grandfather had been in America for years and had sent for her mother, who was then fifteen. But there was no one at the pier to meet her when she finally got to New York after the gruesome Atlantic crossing in steerage. So she just followed the other people, and when no one was left, she sat down on the curb somewhere at Spring and Bleecker streets and cried until some Yiddish-speaking person found her father for her.

Madeline's parents met at an immigrants' dance when they were still in their late teens. Both were handsome and bright, and they were immediately attracted to each other. Otherwise, they were completely incompatible, and thirty years and four children later they were divorced.

While my mother was still making tapioca for sixteen boarders, Madeline's mother showed what a dedicated socialist health nut could do. Other women were boiling the life out of vegetables and chickens, but Madeline's mother's fresh vegetables were cooked just to tender crispness and the Ledermans were the first on the block to eat salads and rare meat. Her kreplach, a sort of Jewish won ton served in hot chicken soup, was famous in five boroughs.

She also had a great sense of humor, but she specialized in sarcasm and in devastating impersonations of people she didn't care for, some of whom her children really liked—and even married.

Both Madeline's parents were needleworkers—her mother a milliner, her father a one-time sewing machine operator who had worked himself up to be a cloak and suit designer. There was a sewing machine open and in use in the house, but none of the children were allowed to touch it. It was as though the parents were afraid that, like in *Sleeping Beauty,* if the needle pierced one of them it would mean being condemned to work in the needle trades and sweatshops as they themselves did.

Madeline had a "bubba," her father's mother, who wore a long black skirt, high laced shoes and a *sheitel,* the wig worn by Orthodox women. A tiny, wiry lady who lived to be eighty, she had nine children. Madeline's father, as the oldest son, had brought the family over to America after he had emigrated and established himself as a sewing machine operator. She must have gone to the same school as my mother, because she also knew a little something about insurance. She'd learned how to bounce off taxicabs on the Grand Concourse on her way to synagogue. After collecting the insurance money, she'd distribute it to several of her daughters—all of whom seemed to have married taxi drivers. None of them could feed their children because little old ladies were always suing their husbands.

Madeline's father was very funny, too, known in his circle as Meshugana Max—crazy Max. He was also a stander. He ate only while standing at the stove. He also stood all day at the cutting table, and after work he stood gossiping on a street corner for a while. Then he stood on the long subway ride from the garment district to the upper reaches of the Bronx. (The trip got longer and longer because every few years Madeline's mother would move the family further uptown in search of "the country.") Maybe standing at the stove gave Madeline's father the running start he needed to get out of the house each night to visit his lady friend, a widow whom he eventually married with the explanation, "Listen, we're going together eighteen years, she's no bum."

Madeline saw her father lie down only once, in a Manhattan hospital where she and her mother had been called by the police. He'd been struck by a hit-and-run driver, and as his head hit the curb he fractured his skull. After they left him, apparently asleep in a turbaned bandage, he got up, dressed, walked out of the hospital, took the subway home (did he sit down, I've always wondered?) and the next day went to work in his turban. He worked every day of his life until, one Saturday morning, he died of a heart attack doing his favorite thing, singing with the radio. He, like my father, loved to sing all the popular songs, and Madeline knows the lyrics of those songs—but in her father's accent. She was fourteen before she realized the "little gray home in de vest" was not a small doll house in her father's vest pocket.

Madeline and her brother and sisters were encouraged to go to the vaudeville show on Sundays at the Audubon Theater. Frances, the oldest daughter, became stage-struck as a result, and when

Madeline was three, Francie began to drag her and ten-year-old Thelma to the Hecksher Foundation's Children's Theatre on 103rd Street and Fifth Avenue. Little Madeline would be plumped into a seat while the older girls actually performed in the theater. One day the boy playing Tiny Tim in *A Christmas Carol* had an accident and Madeline was able to take his place because she knew the lines by heart from sitting for weeks in the auditorium. The 1927 performance of *A Christmas Carol* with Madeline Lee as Tiny Tim was one of the first remote pickups on early radio. With that part, Madeline began her show business career, and she's been on the stage or behind the scenes ever since.

During the summer of 1928 Madeline was entered in a Jean Darling look-alike contest in the Palisades Amusement Park. The judges took a long time to make up their minds, and Madeline refused to leave the stage during their deliberations. She just stood there in the black lace sunsuit her mother had made for her. (Her mother made all her costumes, and recently Madeline brought out the historic sunsuit. It's a minuscule wisp of a garment, decorated with tiny mirror buttons around the neckline. The bottom is made of a lace densely decorated with flowers so that you can't see through it. It should be in a museum, it's so perfect.) Then, as now, the only way to get Madeline off was to let her win. So they did. The prize was to replace Jean Darling in several of the Our Gang comedies, and this led to a part in Jack Benny's first short, *Taxi Tangle,* and the role of Leo Carillo's daughter in a feature film.

The money Madeline made in her shows and movies and in several kiddie acts was put straight into lessons at a famous children's studio headed by a black vocal teacher named Mabel Horsey. Like my mother (and Jack's and Zero's mothers, too), Madeline's mother wanted her daughters to have it easier than she did. As an early feminist, she was determined that they'd have an education and careers so they wouldn't end up as housewives whose only life was in the kitchen. In those days show business seemed a promising way out of poverty.

At Mabel Horsey's the staff was almost entirely black. The rehearsal pianist was an eleven-year-old named Hazel Scott. The only white teacher taught ballet and acrobatics, and the best acrobats in the class were her daughters, known as the Delite Twins. (I told you there were more twins in those days.)

Madeline took singing, piano, tap dancing, ballet and acrobatics. To this day, late at somewhat drunken parties, at no popular request she'll turn a cartwheel or do an impersonation of Ginger Rogers. A psychiatrist she once consulted about this compulsion finally suggested, "Have you ever thought of doing Alice Faye?" Somewhere in those years she also learned "talking," at which she still excels. Her early talking got her a job as the world's youngest girl radio announcer. "The world" was WOV on Forty-third Street on Saturday mornings and WINS on Fifty-eighth Street on Sundays. The program she announced and emceed was *Mabel Horsey's Varieties*, which, while less well known than *The Horn & Hardart Hour*, spawned a lot of good talent, including Hazel Scott and at least two of the leading Dead End Kids, Billy Halop and Bobby Jordan. And, of course, our Madeline. She held the world radio announcer title from the time she was eight until she was sixteen.

Madeline got $5 an hour for the radio programs, and counting the extra dramatic programs she did on Sundays, she, like me, was earning $15 a week as a child performer.

She had been taught to read at age four by Francie, who was practicing to be a teacher, and even as a little kid she could take a quick look at a script and give it a good reading right away. Which came in handy in radio work, the "new" medium Madeline was involved in.

Though none of her lessons at Mabel Horsey's really took, Madeline had a natural and unique style of doing things that set her

61

****
170 YEARS OF SHOW BUSINESS

apart from the group—like starting on the left foot when the rest of the dancers were starting with the right. Observing this special talent, Madeline's mother decided to accentuate the negative. Once she snipped the elastic on Madeline's underpants so that at a strategic moment all eyes would be riveted on the little girl with the panties around her ankles. Another time she purposely reversed a black-and-white costume's design so that Madeline would not only be doing things differently from all the other girls, but it would look as if the differences were planned. Her mother's strategy worked, and Madeline was launched on a career of doing everything a little bit wrong but making it turn out all right in the end.

From the time she was about eight Madeline was a "regular" on *Ray Knight's Coo-Coos,* a radio program which was one of the first to poke fun at radio itself. The show was a take-off on *One Man's Family.* Ray Knight's family consisted of seven children: Monday Knight, Tuesday Knight, Wednesday Knight . . . you get the idea.

Madeline played the next-to-the-youngest, Friday. The baby, Saturday Knight, was played by the real-life Mrs. Ray Knight, who put her face in a pillow and cried like an infant. A quick study, Madeline learned that, too, and she made it her specialty later on in radio, doing babies' and little kids' voices until the early 1950's —by which time she was just a little past baby age.

Incidentally, bearing out my theory about twins, there was a set on that show, too. The Mauch twins were beautiful identical boys who became big stars when they played in *The Prince and the Pauper* in the movies. Madeline had a crush on them both. (So did I.) Years later, when she was a talent coordinator on an industrial movie with Harpo Marx and Mickey Rooney, she met a short, round balding film editor . . . one of the Mauch twins. After the initial shock, she realized that she was now a short, round, though not balding talent coordinator, no longer a cute little blonde with corkscrew curls manufactured nightly by a diligent stage mother.

Tap routines used to be all the rage, especially tapping to classical music. You could buy the routines from a tap teacher—$50 to $100 for a soft shoe, Spanish tap or a rousing number designed for the *Hungarian Rhapsody*. Madeline's mother scrimped from her "table money" to buy Thelma some of those routines, and since she was a clever and frugal person she got Thelma to teach them to Madeline. The girls were sent down to the cement basement to work out because when you lived four flights up you could hardly subject the neighbors below to several hours a day of the *Hungarian Rhapsody* tap dance.

When Madeline got as good as she could get (those lessons didn't take too well, either), she began performing her act at various social functions throughout the five boroughs. Once, after traveling all the way to a Knights of Columbus kiddie show in Brooklyn to do her Spanish tap—complete with shawl and a rose in her baby teeth —she and her mother were shocked to find another young performer prepared to do the number Madeline had planned. Undaunted, Madeline tried out the same steps to the *Hungarian Rhapsody*. They fit perfectly, and with the shawl and rose discarded, the basic peasant Spanish costume became basic peasant Hungarian. For years after, Madeline didn't know whether she'd perform the same steps to *Adios, Muchachos* or the *Hungarian Rhapsody*.

Radio City—where several of us were to spend quite a bit of time—had just been built, and NBC's new studios there were enormous. The second-floor powder rooms were huge mirrored ballrooms that looked like an art deco Versailles. They also contained the first chaise longues Madeline and her mother had ever lain down on. The matron had to leave before the two of them set about figuring out how to sit gracefully on the things. Later, Madeline's mother remembered that some of the neighbors on the Lower East Side had chaise longues, though not as luxury seating in the boudoir. A chaise longue would be used as sleeping accommodations for the newest immigrants, but their version of it came out "Tonight, you sleep on the 'lunch.' "

Madeline's mother's accent was very slight (the family had spoken only Yiddish until the kids brought English home from school), yet she still felt that being Jewish would hold Madeline back in radio. So when she brought Madeline to work or to an audition, she waited outside and was careful not to speak to anyone lest they detect a trace of Yiddish. Actually, there was some anti-Semitism among the actors and sponsors in the studios, though it was confined to offhand remarks. Madeline would sometimes overhear such talk while playing checkers or jacks with other child actors like Leon Janney and Billy Redfield under the big grand piano in the studio. (They called this hideaway "The Private Treehouse in Studio 3B at NBC.")

Madeline's career as a theatrical producer began at Walton High, an all-girls school in the Bronx. In fact, her first production almost prevented her from graduating, though it taught her a lot of lessons she was able to use in the future and eventually she became very busy in that field. Watching her run around town with her purse over her shoulder and three or four canvas bags flapping about her legs, someone once suggested she call herself Shopping Bag Productions. Appearance, however, belies fact: Madeline's brain is a microfilm on which is recorded present and obsolete Equity rules, the entire roster of New York and California actors, and a sure cure for morning sickness.

Born political, when Madeline got to Walton in 1937 Americans were enlisting in the Lincoln Brigade to help defeat Franco in Spain. Japan had invaded China a few years before, and Madeline still remembers weeping at the pictures of Chinese babies crying in the streets of Nanking. She talked politics with the boys she met at the adjacent DeWitt Clinton Boys' High School. I talked sports with the boys I met at West Philly. I was discussing with my boyfriends why Schoolboy Rowe was leaving the major leagues while Madeline was breaking up with a boy over the Nazi-Soviet pact.

But before that argument this same boy inadvertently got Madeline launched as a producer. He suggested that she join the American Student Union, an anti-fascist peace group. The chapter at Walton had only sixteen members, and they met, literally, underground, in someone's basement, because open anti-fascism was not allowed in a public high school.

Madeline to this day is no great shakes at math, but it doesn't take an Einstein to figure out that sixteen girls weren't going to make much of a dent on the war against fascism. She decided to mount her first "show" as a way of attracting membership to the group. She and three other ASU members handed out leaflets worded in the following political way: "Come and learn all about syphilis with the DeWitt Clinton Boys." Madeline Lee, fledgling producer, had arranged for the Board of Health to send their traveling lecturer and a venereal disease film to a room she had rented near the school. Her DeWitt Clinton friend had invited *that* student body, and the event promised to be the highlight of the social season.

Over 300 girls attended, and at the end of the meeting eighty signed up for membership in the ASU. Even this expansion didn't stop war and fascism—as later events have made clear—but it wasn't a total loss. Two of the girls married boys they met at that meeting.

Out of all this, Madeline earned a reputation as some species of "red menace." When she was only fourteen, her activities as an ASU agitator brought her first subpoena from the Rapp-Coudert Committee, a New York State legislative group that was a kind of precursor of the House Un-American Activities Committee. Because she was underage she didn't have to accept the subpoena, but I think she would have given them a run for their money even then.

65

****
170 YEARS OF SHOW BUSINESS

It didn't take long before the young principal of Walton called Madeline into her office to explain that the ASU was a nefarious organization with international affiliations and that Madeline would do better joining the dramatic society or the debating club. Madeline was already involved in both, and she rather liked the ASU's affiliations since they meant she got to go to conventions out of town. She had met a lovely English boy at the World Youth Festival dance. She told the principal how much the ASU meant to her.

The principal then wanted the name of the ASU's faculty adviser. While this interview was basic training for her later political life, Madeline was only fifteen by then and not yet adept at dealing with cagey questions. She let the name slip. This was the first and last time she ever finked, but the poor faculty adviser was promptly transferred.

In her senior year Madeline began to feel increased pressure from the principal, who now wanted the entire ASU membership list so she could make out scholarship recommendations. Without this information, she said pointedly, no one could get into college. Madeline hadn't planned to go to college anyhow. Paying for it was out of the question, and for free tuition at the city colleges you needed an 86.4 average. Madeline had majored in ASU and had already failed the math Regents three times. She'd gone to summer school and found a nice neighbor to help her with her math homework, but college wasn't really on her mind. (In fact, the neighbor was, but that's another story.)

As graduation neared, the principal laid it on the line: Madeline was not going to graduate because she had not fulfilled the "character requirements."

Madeline accepted this but went ahead with all the normal things you do when you're about to graduate. She worked on the yearbook, took the same rotten cap-and-gown picture as the rest of the kids, was in the senior play and went to the senior prom, necked in a car afterwards and pressed her corsage in the yearbook.

Then, very peculiarly, she got an invitation to the graduation. It was held in Carnegie Hall, and Madeline was surprised to find that her seat was in the "prizewinners' row." Without even trying, she had won the Jesse W. Yanowitz Memorial Award for the Student with the Most Perseverance and Conscientious Endeavor in Social Science. She *had* to graduate. Madeline was flabbergasted. She had gotten good grades in social science and remembered taking some kind of oral exam, but she never thought she'd win a prize. And a prize with $100 attached to it! Madeline figures the four teachers who judged the oral exam were so afraid she might make even more trouble if she didn't graduate that they gave her the prize to get her out of Walton.

Madeline's antics as ASU president at Walton came to the attention of the members of the City College ASU chapter, which was putting on a show called *Pens and Pencils*—a political revue styled after the International Ladies Garment Workers' famous *Pins and Needles*. When the City College group heard that Madeline was an actress as well as an activist, Marvin Rothenberg, the producer-director with whom she's worked ever since, invited her to assist him.

Madeline's first task was to pick up the songs and sketches from the writers who had been assigned to the show. Much of the material was written by talented students, but some faculty members also contributed. One of these was Earl Robinson, who was to write *Ballad for Americans* and *The House I Live In* with Lewis Allen, who was in reality Abel Meerepole—a DeWitt Clinton teacher who much later, with his wife, adopted the sons of Ethel and Julius Rosenberg after the execution. Abel's most famous song, "Strange Fruit," was introduced in *Pens and Pencils*. The song was to make

****

Billie Holiday famous when she introduced it at Cafe Society Downtown, where she shared a dressing room with comedian Jack Gilford. You see how everything is coming together?

Actually, some of the best writing talent in the country contributed to *Pens and Pencils:* Joe Darion (who later wrote *Man of La Mancha*), John LaTouche *(Cabin in the Sky, Golden Apple),* Sam Locke *(Fair Game),* David Shaw *(Redhead)* and Frank Tarloff *(Father Goose).*

The show also attracted great performers, though it took three strong people to force Pete Seeger onto the stage of City College's 1,200-seat theater. Irwin Corey, on the other hand, was not shy. It took three people to get him *off* the stage after his first performance. The team of Martin Ross and Bernie West—cleverly billed as Ross and West—were the comedy act. (Bernie grew up to be a producer and writer on *All in the Family.*) Madeline performed some sketches with Ross and West but they made their biggest hits on their own, winning the *Major Bowes Amateur Hour* contest and playing the Paramount in New York. During the war they split up and Bernie found himself a new partner, who changed his name to Mickey Ross so the team wouldn't have to change their posters or stationery. When poor Martin Ross returned to show business, he found his name had been taken. So he became Ross Martin. Madeline keeps that sort of thing in her head, and I set it down here to show that although she's no longer a child actress, her mind is still agile.

Madeline was still in high school, of course, but when *Pens and Pencils* became a big hit and toured the Eastern college circuit, she decided she really wanted to do more theater. She joined the New Theatre League, which was similar to today's off-Broadway theater. The NTL had an acting school, and there Madeline met Stanley Prager, Josh Shelley and a girl named Shirley Shrift. When Shirley changed her name to Shelley Winters, Josh said, "Well, that does it. We can't get married. That would make you Shelley Shelley."

Madeline also joined an acting group at Schiff Center, a synagogue in the Bronx where she met Martin Balsam. After they'd played Sid and Florry together in Clifford Odets' *Waiting for Lefty*, Madeline and Marty formed their own revue troupe and did topical material and serious readings around the Bronx. They rehearsed at Madeline's house—often with such dedication that Madeline's mother would find them on the couch at two in the morning, still rehearsing and expressing their love for the theater.

Every one of their friends was insatiable for the theater but also hungry for food, and they were all too poor to gratify both needs. When they could, they got 55¢ tickets in the balcony, but most of the time they didn't have that much between them. So they devised their own system of subsidized theatergoing-plus-eating. With their coats over their shoulders, they'd mingle with the intermission crowd and go back in for the second and third act of everything on Broadway. To this day they've never seen the first acts of any of the plays of that period. Needless to say, they had stumbled on the way improvident New Yorkers have attended the theater since the Nieu Amsterdam Follies.

Madeline's group added a touch of its own, however. They'd meander over to the Hotel Diplomat or some other hotel in the Broadway area and track down whatever wedding or bar mitzvah reception was being held. (Of course, they were careful to pick out Jewish or Italian weddings, since at WASP affairs they'd get nothing but small portions of wedding cake and maybe a drop of domestic champagne.) Balancing a knish or ravioli in one hand, a member of the strolling troupe of players, pretending to be from the bride or groom's side, would saunter up to a nice uncle or a friendly-looking sister-in-law:

"So, how is Sol?"

"Is Aunt Rosa's hip better?"

"What, Murray isn't working yet? What's Goldie doing?"

Though not exactly Stanislavski's Method, it was their own and they ate well.

Madeline, in the meantime, had become very involved with her mathematical neighbor, Mitchell Fein. They'd met in an elevator in the building where they both lived with their parents. Madeline was sixteen; Mitch was seven years older and a graduate in engineering from NYU. A grown-up man.

Mitch's family welcomed Madeline in spite of their concern about her being so young. But Madeline's mother took a very tough and forbidding attitude toward Mitchell. She wouldn't even give her permission for Madeline to spend a weekend at the Feins' summer bungalow on Lake Mohegan. Madeline told her mother she was staying at a girlfriend's house and went anyway. When she arrived, she discovered that her mother had no reason to worry: she found herself pinned at night into a double bed between Mitch's mother and his robust aunt.

But young people in love will find a way. Mitch took Madeline out for a ride in his sailboat. She was wearing a pair of yellow bib-topped overalls—and what do you know? They got becalmed out in the middle of this big lake. It was very hot. There was all this water. Who could blame Madeline for rolling up her pants legs and dangling her feet over the side? And—it could happen to anyone—the water lapped up at her legs and her overalls got soaked. Anyone would have done what she did—take off the wet overalls and hang them up like a flag on the mast to dry. Who could have predicted that just then a little breeze would come up and that the little vessel would begin to start heading swiftly and arrow-like for the shore?

As luck would have it, standing on the pier and waving wildly as the little boat came into view was Madeline's mother with her sister Fran. Someone had figured out that Madeline was not at her girlfriend's, and she'd been traced to this very spot.

The overalls were waving in the breeze. Madeline was not exactly dressed to receive company, and her mother had the incriminating evidence, the proof positive, that Mitchell Fein was out to seduce her innocent little girl. They gathered Madeline into the car, and she spent the night in Fran's bungalow in Rye, New York, while her mother alternated between tirades about morality and bribes to keep her from running off with Mitch.

Mitchell and Madeline were married in a small ceremony at a synagogue in the Bronx. Madeline's mother didn't attend. She'd gone to sunny Florida, having announced her intention to commit suicide. She didn't talk to Madeline for eighteen months after the wedding. But Madeline's father came, bringing her a gift of one of the first fake furs. It was made into a little jacket and formed part of the wedding ensemble. Madeline describes it as imitation hamster, but it had the highfalutin name of Baronadukey. Her wedding dress, in the great tradition of ugly matrimonial attire, was a rerun made of leftover upholstery material. She carried a chrysanthemum in a hue to blend with the Baronadukey.

At first the young couple stayed on in the Bronx. Madeline continued with her radio work and commuted nearly every day to Manhattan, where she worked in soap operas like *Our Gal Sunday*, *The Second Mrs. Burton* and *Portia Faces Life*, as well as Norman Corwin's dramas. She did comedy when Eddie Cantor or Jack Benny came to New York with their long-running radio shows. And once she appeared on *The Chamber Music Society of Lower Basin Street*, where she first met Zero.

At the time, Zero needed comedy material, and by coincidence a friend of Madeline's, a Bronx social worker named Joe Stein, had been dabbling in writing comedy. Zero bought Joe's first sketch, and pretty soon Joe was writing lots of material for radio, including

The Henry Morgan Show, on which Madeline was now a regular. One of Joe's most famous sketches for the show was about Ludwig von Beethoven, who, it was said, developed a composing block and was uninspired for weeks. While he sat at the piano, his head in his hands, his faithful wife (Madeline) brought him food and dusted the piano keys. One day, at her work, she sang a little melody that went something like *du-du-du-dummm.* "That's it!" cried Ludwig. "I'll call it *The Fifth Symphony.*"

Later, Joe Stein, that former social worker–comedy writer, wrote the book for a play called *Fiddler on the Roof.*

When she heard that Maxwell Anderson's *The Eve of St. Mark* needed a replacement, she applied in one of her father's finest tailored outfits and didn't even get an audition. One of the lessons she teaches would-be actresses today is: If you're reading for the part of a floozy, don't dress like Mrs. Miniver! The day after, she slunk into the room in a red dress cut down to the navel, got a reading and was hired.

When the show had completed its Broadway run, it was toured by Jules J. Leventhal, the colorful and notoriously stingy producer of the subway circuit. Somewhere between the Flatbush Theater and the Washington Heights Audubon, Madeline's bright green shoes, which must have cost all of $3.98, were lost. Madeline went on that night, her size 5 feet and some tissue paper stuffed into size 7 shoes. The next day she said to Leventhal, "Do you want to spend three ninety-eight or replace me with someone who can fit into these shoes?"

When a new girl came into the show, on the first day's rehearsal Leventhal, standing in the back of the theater with the stage manager, said, "I can't hear her."

"What do you care?" said the stage manager. "She stinks."

"I know," Leventhal replied, "but for my money I like to hear her stink."

This has become another maxim Madeline teaches her students, and both of us consider it the first rule of the theater:

"Let them hear you stink."

Madeline developed another uncanny talent. She managed to get "big name" signatures on petitions for the causes she and her friends in Equity and AFTRA were interested in. Her system? She simply went to every Broadway stage door. She had friends in supporting roles or bit parts in nearly every play, and she got them to get the names of the stars. Her anti–poll tax petitions would have turned a stage-door autograph hound green with envy. Phil Loeb and Sam Jaffe began to take notice of the dizzy blonde with the hot political blood in her veins.

One name on her Equity list gave her more trouble than usual. She simply couldn't find a guy named Jerome Robbins. Then at a benefit dance, while Madeline was doing a lindy hop with an actor friend, she felt a tap on her shoulder.

"Pardon me," said the thin, young, handsome man, "would you teach me that dance you're doing? My name is Jerome Robbins and I have a special reason for wanting to learn it."

Madeline was thunderstruck. "Aren't you a member of Equity?"

She didn't know that Jerome Robbins was an unusually gifted choreographer on the threshold of his first success. She didn't care. She wanted him to sign one of her petitions. *Then* she'd teach him the lindy hop. He signed and she showed him how the dance was done.

Robbins was being given his first big chance, to choreograph a full-length ballet for Ballet Theatre. It was the story of three sailors on leave in New York and it was to be called *Fancy Free*. Robbins had lived for too long in the cloistered world of ballet to have any idea of the "street" dances real sailors would do. With sources like Madeline he learned how to lindy, and we've all seen the results. *Fancy Free* was adapted by Adolph Green, Betty Comden and Leonard Bernstein, and played in the movies and on Broadway as *On the Town*. Madeline was offered a nice, funny part in that play by Robbins, but she was trying to get into the Theatre Guild production *Embezzled Heaven* with Ethel Barrymore and Albert Basserman.

She had tried unsuccessfully for weeks to get a reading of the coveted part of a sixteen-year-old kitchen maid in a Czech castle. (Ethel Barrymore played the cook.) Now, it happened that the Theatre Guild was holding simultaneous auditions for their American folk musical, *Sing Out, Sweet Land*. As an Equity member, Madeline could automatically audition at the open chorus call. Though she really had no interest in the show, she did audition—but dressed as a European peasant girl and singing a simple European folk song.

The casting director, who had managed to elude Madeline's photographs and pleas, now came running down the aisle: "Listen, I'm sorry. You're not right for this show, but come and read for *Embezzled Heaven.*"

She got the part and that's how a little girl from the Bronx came to play in the cast with one of the most famous actresses of the American theater.

Madeline was frankly scared to death of Miss Barrymore, but it turned out that Barrymore always felt drawn to the sympathetic characters in her plays. One day, seated in a large circle at the regular afternoon tea break (a Barrymore custom), Madeline heard her stage name "Zdenka" being called. It was the great lady herself, summoning Madeline to her side.

"My dear," she said, "my father always traveled with animals, and I have cut two pictures out of today's rotogravure section because they remind me of you. I can't make up my mind if you are as cute as this kitten or this monkey."

That melted Madeline's fear and they became good friends.

When Barrymore realized Madeline was never around for the final curtain call because she was off doing some radio show or other, she hired her for her own weekly show, *Miss Hattie.*

Albert Basserman's wife Else had a tiny part in *Embezzled Heaven.* The newspaper *PM* had a review of the play the day after it opened and the headline ran: EMBEZZLED HEAVEN HAS ETHEL BARRYMORE AND LITTLE ELSE. At first, Madeline thought Mrs. Basserman had become an overnight star.

Once, during the run, when Madeline was collecting money backstage for the Independent Citizens Committee to Reelect Franklin Delano Roosevelt, Miss Barrymore called her into herself's dressing room.

"Why didn't you ask me?" she demanded. "Don't you know I'm on the committee?"

Madeline said, "Yes, and that's why I thought it presumptuous to ask you."

Ethel Barrymore replied, "Don't be silly, here's a hundred dollars, and if you find out how much my brother, Lionel, gave Thomas E. Dewey, I'll double it!"

Another Barrymore encounter took place when Madeline cut her finger onstage while slicing lemons for a scene. She brought Miss Barrymore the sliced lemons on a plate with her bleeding finger. Barrymore's next line was to ask her to bring some parsley, but she stared at the plate.

"Zdenka," she said, "go in the garden and get me a plate of blood." Later in the play, she solicitously pulled Madeline to the corner of the stage.

"Are you hurt?" she asked—and *not* in a stage whisper. She seemed incapable of lowering that magnificent voice. She started waving her wooden cooking spoon into the wings in the direction of the stage manager. "I'll bring down the curtain if you're hurt."

Madeline wound her stage apron tightly around her finger to stop the bleeding—and Miss Barrymore. She still has a tiny scar and ridged nail on her left forefinger to show for it, but that seems to me an easier souvenir to show than my ballet dancer's bunions.

Embezzled Heaven had a decent run before it closed when Ethel Barrymore developed pneumonia. That was her last Broadway appearance.

At about that time Madeline and Mitch moved to Manhattan, and Mitch mounted a campaign to get Madeline more work in daytime radio so that she could be home in the evenings. An efficiency expert, he drafted a publicity campaign of picture post cards, which they sent out to every radio producer in New York. Before long Madeline had more work than she'd ever had before.

The Feins were conveniently located on Fifty-seventh Street, and their apartment became a central meeting place. In 1943 the nominating committee of Actors Equity failed to put Phil Loeb up for another term as a member of the Equity Council, and everyone who was liberal, progressive or just nice gathered at the apartment to help form an independent slate. (In addition to her organizing ability and her central location, Madeline was the only actress anybody knew who had access to a Mimeograph machine—Mitchell's. Five years later, when Mitch and Madeline got divorced, Phil Loeb's first question was "Who got custody of the Mimeograph machine?").

It was during the Phil Loeb emergency campaign that Madeline and I met. She was everything I wanted to be: small, cute, blue-eyed. She was also working and married. But it was her amazing domestic efficiency that impressed me that first night. She was preparing dinner for the usual crowd of thirty ravenous show business people. Her living room was filled with a milling throng, and she was in the kitchen calmly taking everything, from appetizer to dessert, out of the refrigerator and piling it on the counter. "That way you only have to open the door once," she explained. I think of it every time I cook dinner.

•   •   •

76

****

MOSTEL/GILFORD

When it looked like the war was almost over, Madeline and Mitch decided to have a baby, but unfortunately she lost it during pregnancy. Then, about a year later, she gave birth to her first child, Lisa.

In the meantime, they'd moved to Eighty-first Street. The place had been designed by the same architect who'd done Radio City Music Hall. Made me feel right at home. The living room was two stories high and had a balcony about halfway up where you could sit and look down into a sunken area that reminded some of us very much of the Music Hall stage. The whole room was done in art deco style. The walls were hung with yards and yards of Dan River fabric. Gorgeous. It was the perfect setting for the kind of party we all used to have, where show people would entertain for a good cause.

At one such party Madeline Lee Fein met Jack Gilford, who had come to perform. Like many married people, Madeline couldn't stand to see anyone single. Jack was not only unmarried, he had *never been* married. It was 1947, and there were lots of single people around in our crowd. Jack didn't really need any help meeting girls, but he somehow had avoided getting hooked.

Madeline began a relentless campaign to get Jack married off, introducing him to all her nicest and prettiest friends. Jack obediently began going out with them. Finally, she realized that she'd done such a good job selling Jack, she'd sold herself. She thought herself happily married, but there it was. She was in love with Jack, and he was in love with her. Although Jack didn't approve of going around with married ladies, they kept bumping into each other wherever they went.

They met one night when Madeline was wearing only a large wooden barrel representing UNEMPLOYMENT at a benefit for Henry Wallace at Cafe Society Downtown. A barrel's distance apart, they were nevertheless soon deeply involved in one of their usual intense discussions. At some point, Madeline told him what men tradition-

★★

ally say to women: "Don't get any ideas that this is going to lead anywhere. We're just going to have a nice uncomplicated relationship."

But it got complicated, so Mitchell and Jack had one of those man-to-man talks and Jack agreed with Mitchell that it would have to stop. Jack didn't see himself as a home-breaker. He saw himself as a nice guy and decided to put more than a barrel's distance between them. He took a job at Green Mansions, a summer resort in the Adirondacks with a famous theater.

The night he was leaving, he took Madeline to a restaurant for a farewell dinner. Though she was furious that he and Mitchell had decided her future for her, she couldn't get him to change his mind. He did agree to drive her to a union caucus on his way out of town, but on Fortieth Street and First Avenue the car had a flat and Madeline had to hail a cab. She was at the meeting only a few minutes when she bolted from the room and headed straight back to Fortieth Street, where Jack and two garage mechanics were still struggling with the tire. Madeline had seen enough Jean Arthur movies to know what to do next. In front of the bewildered mechanics she threw herself into Jack's arms. And when he finally went off into the distance, with the lights cutting through the fog on the East River, she had his promise that she could come see him at Green Mansions and that he'd call her whenever he could.

Every night that summer Jack, armed with a pocketful of change, would enter a phone booth in the Adirondacks and call Madeline. She had left Mitch, and with $750 she had made in soap operas she bought a divorce in Arkansas. Now she could say to Jack, "I'm no longer a married woman, so you're no longer a home-breaker." She spent the summer begging him not to return to Brooklyn but to move in with her when he came back. And serving as a liaison for the young lovers was the evening telephone operator of that little mountain town who, in the tradition of her profession, would listen in on their passion and tears. It was her own closed-circuit soap opera. One night, when Jack as usual asked at the end of the evening's tragic dialogue, "How much do I owe you?" a voice sobbed back, "Never mind. There's no charge tonight."

It was during this period that Madeline came under the spell of E. Y. "Yip" Harburg and his wife Edelaine, who were Jack's close friends. When someone suggested that the song Jack sang in *The Wallace Show*—a Durante imitation ("I votes for him, I votes for him/I irritates the tonsils of my troats for him")—should be made into a 16mm movie, Madeline had called Yip, who had written the song, and got Eddie on the phone instead.

"Aren't you the girl who's going with Jack Gilford?" Eddie asked. And when Madeline owned up to the fact, Eddie said, "You should marry him, you know."

That was only the first of many insane suggestions that Eddie has made to Madeline over the years. Madeline always follows her advice. She can't help it. As she says, "Eddie is some kind of Jewish Transylvanian and I'm her Finklestein."

Eventually Edelaine Harburg became the Gilford children's godmother and Yip the godfather as well as the official family poet. For Madeline's fiftieth birthday party he wrote "The Ballad of Madeline Lee," which includes these lines:

> *She dwells in the Village*
>   *In Abingdon Square*
> *The beautiful Madeline Lee*
> *All telephone wires converge*
>   *On her there*
> *The sweetheart of AT&T.*
> *You ask who she is? She's the soul of the city,*
> *The sweetie committed to every committee*
> *The wife of Jack Gilford, the funny, the witty*
>   *The bountiful Madeline Lee*

In that "Summer of Green Mansions," Madeline would fly to the resort in a tiny Adirondacks Airline plane. Her father was still outfitting her with stylish suits. Imagine, if you will, Madeline in perfectly tailored white gabardine, her hair blowing in the wind on the airfield, waiting for Jack to pick her up—as Ingrid Bergman in *Casablanca*. And Jack's resolve began to weaken.

It took a while, however, for Madeline to get to be the aforementioned "wife of Jack Gilford." If he'd thought about it, he would have realized that the thing was really a *fait accompli* months before, when, at a Village restaurant, he first noticed a peculiar look in Madeline's eyes. It was the look of Madeline with her mind made up—in this instance, to marry him. Jack describes it as the expression seen on the face of an eager German shepherd. He's accustomed to it now, but he used to think that when she got that look, two men in white coats would come and say, "She's a very nice person but she does get these ideas. You just sit there and we'll take her away." But no one took her away, and now there are three offspring whose eyebrows get the same determined shepherd dog slant.

When Green Mansions closed at the end of the summer, Jack sent his camp trunk to the apartment Madeline found for them in Greenwich Village because that's where Jack had idly once said he would like to live. Jack says they "ad lived" there for about six months. On April 6, 1949, after Madeline's divorce from Mitch was final, they got married.

The next step was getting custody of Madeline's little girl, Lisa, whom she'd had to leave with Mitch. The referee at the custody proceedings was an ancient retired jurist. The hearings dragged on and on, with lots of testimony to Madeline's fine character and Jack's virtues. At one point the old gentleman rapped the desk with his gavel and said, "Jack, Jack, Jack. I'm tired of hearing about Jack."

In his chambers he announced his decision. "I don't like any of these people," he said, "but a little girl should be with her mother."

Mitchell, however, wasn't willing to give Lisa up, and so, on the afternoon of the opening night of *Alive and Kicking*, Jack and Madeline, summoned by a friend who lived in the building, went to Eighty-first Street to repossess the child. I have never understood the logistics, which would take a military tactician to map, but somehow Madeline ended up passing Lisa and a doll almost the same size as a two-year-old through the kitchen window to where Jack was waiting for her.

Jack and Lisa were already great friends. Once, when she was old enough to write her name, Jack got her to sign a statement that said, "I am having a happy childhood." Because Mitchell saw a lot of Lisa, too, Jack dubbed him his husband-in-law.

Madeline's aforementioned German shepherd look returned one night when she was pregnant with the Gilfords' first son, Joe. She sat up in bed, and her eyebrows came together at the center, and she said, "I have a wonderful idea." By that time the look and the steamroller that followed would make Jack sweat in places he'd never sweated before—behind his ears and at the sides of his nose. This time she came up with a dilly.

"Look," she said, "this apartment is too small. Lisa is sleeping in the only bedroom, we're in the living room and where are we going to put this baby?"

Jack agreed that the place was too small, but it wasn't easy to find an apartment in New York then.

"What we'll do is this," said the steamroller. "We'll get the people next-door to move out. Then we'll break through the wall between the apartments, and we'll have eight rooms instead of three."

Jack decided if he didn't say another word the idea would be gone by morning. Pregnant women have their whims.

By morning Madeline had drawn up the floor plan and decided on the color scheme for the new living room. But first there was this family that needed relocating—even if they didn't know it.

She marched next-door and told the people innocently living there that she knew of a wonderful place on Eighty-first Street that they'd like a lot better than where they were now living. In fact, her friend Marvin Rothenberg was thinking of moving out of his Eighty-first Street apartment but he had an $800 dining room set that was too big to move. So—Madeline and Jack bought the table and chairs and sold them for only a little less than they had paid, and Madeline talked the people next-door into moving out. They were a nice couple, and they probably didn't know what hit them.

Jack worried about asking the landlord to let them knock down one of his walls. Madeline said: "Let's not mention it to him."

They called in the demolition squad, and as the building shook and the whole neighborhood reverberated, the wall—a fire wall, eight inches thick and built to last—came tumbling down.

When it was all done, Jack was summoned to talk to the landlord. One of the other tenants had blabbed. Contrary to Jack's fears, all the landlord wanted was a $150 deposit in case he had to replace the wall for the next tenant. Rather than forfeit the money, the Gilfords, to this day, live in that apartment.

Jack calls this episode the day he and Madeline invented stonewalling.

By the time Joe and his brother Sam were born, Madeline's mother was the only grandparent left alive and she was not your Jewish-grandmotherly type. Her neurotic pride in her own children excluded all others, even her grandchildren. But though she barely tolerated her daughter-in-law and her other sons-in-law, she adored

Jack. When he went to Hollywood, where she now lived, she cooked him some of her great gefilte fish, her kreplach and her very special butter cookies. She waited at the window for him all day. While he ate, she scolded him for not marrying Madeline before Mitch did, and he assured her he wouldn't have been interested in a seventeen-year-old girl.

Still, the Gilford children really had no local, loving grand-parents, and Jack felt this was like a missing vitamin. Joe especially was crazy about old people and would hang around them as they sat on benches in the park. Once, after Jack had seen him ask an old man to lift him up to a water fountain, he decided his son should no longer be deprived of a grandfather. So Grampa Max began to show up. Jack had only to say to Joe, "C'mon, you vant to go to de park today? I'll buy you a malted. Or do you vant a pencil box or a pen viper?" Joe would immediately fall into the improvisation, treating Jack as his grampa. Jack would literally turn into an old man the way he does on the stage playing Crouch in *Sly Fox*, and he'd say, "C'mon, you'll go on the slide and burn your pants. Vot you vant to do? Box? C'mon, Jack Dempsey. Hey, to a grampa you give an uppercut? And don't call me Gramps. I'm a grandfather, not a disease." The kids loved it.

Twenty years later, Joe's senior film at the NYU film school was a seventeen-minute short called *Max*. Grampa had become an old Palace Theatre Stage Door Man, but it was still Jack playing the old man—though now his son was directing him.

(By the way, Toby Mostel was a "consultant art director" on the film, which is the only student short ever to have had a regular six-week engagement at Radio City Music Hall. Notice how often we end up or begin at the Music Hall?

And Lisa named her little boy, the Gilfords' first grandchild, Max.)

Jack Gilford, like Zero, Madeline and me, was lucky enough to have a mother who was a terribly ambitious, imaginative, strong lady. Maybe a sociologist could tell us what it was about those days that turned the women into such go-getters. The men worked hard to make a living for their families, but it was Madeline's bubba and my mother who took the insurance companies for a lot of money. It was Zero's mother, not his father, who got the family back to New York and "culture." Without her mother pushing her, Madeline might have remained in the Bronx handing out leaflets; her mother practically threw her out of her highchair and onto the stage. I might have stayed in Philadelphia and married one of the boarders, but my mother wouldn't let me; she also pushed me out into the world.

Of all our mothers, Jack's was really the most colorful. He once thought Susska's life would make a wonderful play called *The Lady from Williamsburg.* The story asks the question, "Can a nice, divorced Jewish lady from Brooklyn raise her children by being a bootlegger?" The time is prohibition, in the late 1920's, and through special arrangement with Jack we've got the story of his mother as he wrote it:

84

****

MOSTEL/GILFORD

"All this took place in the Williamsburg section of Brooklyn. We moved there from the Lower East Side of Manhattan, where I was born. Crossing over was considered a step up the ladder, but if the Lower East Side was considered an *underprivileged* slum, Williamsburg was a better class of slum.

"Our family consisted of my parents, one older and one younger brother, and me, and we lived in Williamsburg during the surge of prosperity which followed World War I and during the Depression years. In our neighborhood the difference between those two economic eras was as invisible as the international date line. The only sign of prosperity we had was the loud voice of the lumpen Republicans. 'Ain't we got prosperity?' they insisted. It made little difference to us. At that time someone must have decided that people weren't suffering enough, so prohibition was invented to further increase the burden on the workingman.

"My parents separated, and since my father wasn't able to help us financially, my mother worked in a local cloak and suit shop as a 'findisher.' She was pretty flashy with the needle. She was also pretty sharp about ways to make ends meet.

"She used to say that hunger embarrassed her, especially in children, more especially in her own children. Some people, she said, believed in Christianity or Judaism or Capitalism. She believed in Not Starving. So she was always on the lookout for a way to increase her small income.

"One day in the shop, while she was 'findishing' with her rapier-like needle and the presser was pounding and gliding his hissing steam iron over the scorched canvas, he recited a recipe for my mother. This was not a formula for making a new kind of cheap no-meat casserole. It was a recipe for a simple mash, a fermentation of potatoes and/or prunes, sugar and water. With this recipe, he said, it was not only possible but absolutely unavoidable that you would come out with a fairly nonpoisonous whiskey. The presser said

1. *Kate's mother, Anna Harkin (right), and her sister Margaret—to whom she stopped talking soon after this picture was taken.*
2. *Kate's father, Hugh J. Harkin, left, with a turn-of-the-century friend nobody ever knew.*
3. *The fat one is not Zero but his brother Velvel, now known as Bill.*

4. *Kate (right) and Joan McCracken. Note the nice curve of the back drape buttressed by Mrs. McCracken.*
5. *Kate as Marilyn Miller with cupid-bow lips.*
6. *Madeline was an early tap dancer. She's at about the same dancing level now.*

7. *Madeline and Ethel Barrymore onstage in* Embezzled Heaven.
8. *Jack and Murray with their mother, Susska. Jack is the pretty blond with the curls.*
9. *In the film* Before Morning, *1933, Madeline got an early start on the telephone.*

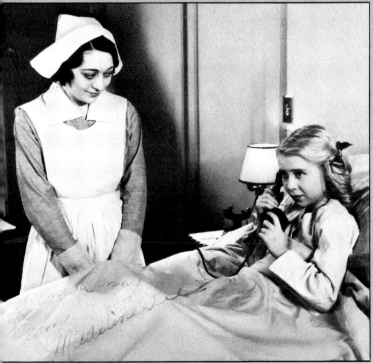

10

12

11

10. At three and a half, Madeline
was carried onto the stage as
Tiny Tim. Her sister Thelma
is on the far left, sister Fran
on the far right.
11. Kate, second from left,
in Broadway Varieties
with an Emmons twin
on each end.
12. Portrait of the artist
as a very young man.
13. In his
intellectual
phase, teaching
on the WPA.

13

MARTIN HARRIS

14

14. Zero, *whose dress was never
to improve, at rehearsal
with* Teddy Wilson
at Cafe Society.
15. Jack *at Cafe Society
in* 1939 *doing*
The Butler
Did It.

15

GRAPHIC HOUSE, INC.

6

17

16. "Millard Fillmore is dead. Nobody came to the funeral."
17. The Senator asking, "What the hell was Hawaii doing in the Pacific?"

18. Jack explaining to the
Cafe Society audience
that "early in its
history, Swing
went under
the name of
Shapiro."

18

19

19. Kate is the fan dancer on
the far right, but, unlike
the custom of the times,
she has clothes on
underneath.
20. Our heroine as
a ballet dancer.

20

21. Working out on the Île de
France, *returning from a*
ballet tour of Europe.
22. Modeling at $5 a day
in Atlantic City.
23. *Madeline, the blonde*
on the right, doing her
bit for the war
effort.

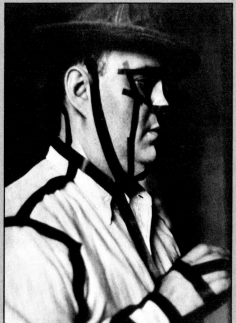

24

25

26

27

24. Zero as Roualt.
25. As a Cézanne self-portrait.
26. As a Matisse odalisque.
27. Zero, Lou Paley,
Shepherd Traub
(the producer)
and Sam Jaffe,
dancing.

ROBERT WILLHEIM

28

29

30

28. *Jack as Bontche Schweig with Ruby Dee in* The World of Sholem Aleichem.
29. *With Patrice Munsel in* Fledermaus, 1950.
30. *The Smoking Sketch, with Carl Reiner, in* Alive and Kicking.

31

32

31. Zero, Jack and Sono Osato in
Once Over Lightly—which
the critics treated heavily.
32. King Sextimus the Silent
in Once upon a Mattress.
33. The Tenth Man,
1959.

33

RUTH ORKIN

34   35

34. *Phil Loeb.*   35. *Taking the A train with Sam Jaffe.*
36. Three Men on a Horse: *Kathryn Cecelia Harkin, Wally Cox
and Walter Matthau.*

36

37

37. *With Carroll O'Connor in the
downtown production of* Ulysses.
38. *In ecstasy over his latest painting.*
39. *During filming of* The Great
Catherine—*"Would you buy
a used car from this man?"*

38

39

40. *Onstage in* Forum.
41. *With Eli Wallach in the 1961*
production of Rhinoceros.
42. *"Waiting for Godot" in*
the 1959 TV performance
with Burgess Meredith,
Alvin Epstein and
Kurt Kasznar.

UNITED ARTISTS

43

43. *Jack, Zero and Buster Keaton on the film set in Spain, 1965.*
44. *Jack finally gets a word in. Bald head is Buster's.*

44

45

45. *"Comedy Tonight."*

46. *The closest the Mostels ever came to a family portrait.*
47. *The real Jack Gilford as pictured in a* New York Times TV *commercial.*

48. *Jack Benny visiting location in Spain. Phil Silvers is on the left.*

49. With Fred Gwynne, Helen
Hayes and Lillian Gish in a
1968 TV production of
Arsenic and Old Lace.
50. With Lotte Lenya
in Cabaret.

COPYRIGHT © 1970
PARAMOUNT PICTURES CORPORATION

51

52

53

51. With Mike Nichols on the set of Catch-22.
52. Doc Daneeka in Catch-22.
53. Yip Harburg and Jack at Madeline's
fiftieth birthday party.

JOSEPH ABELES STUDIO

54

54. *Scene from* Fiddler.
55.*With Jan Kadar and
Harry Belafonte in*
The Angel Levine.
*Zero and Harry
have exchanged
hair.*
56. *Unrestrained
happiness the
morning after
the* Fiddler
opening.

55

56

JOSEPH ABELES STUDIO

57

58

57. Scene from Fiddler.
58. Recording "If I
Were a Rich Man."
59. Scene from
Fiddler.

59

JOSEPH ABELES STUDIO

60

60. *Ruby Keeler and Jack Gilford*
co-star in No, No, Nanette.
61. *Our hero as Tipsy Intruder*
in The David Frost Revue.
62. *Big moment as*
caricature is
hung at
Sardi's.

61

62

63. Monhegan Harbor.
64. A family verdict
with Herbie Kallem.
65. Jack's birthday
party, 1972.

66

66. With Jessie White,
Carroll O'Connor,
Cloris Leachman
and Jim Backus
in a TV special of
Of Thee I Sing.
67. With Jack
Lemmon in
Save the
Tiger.

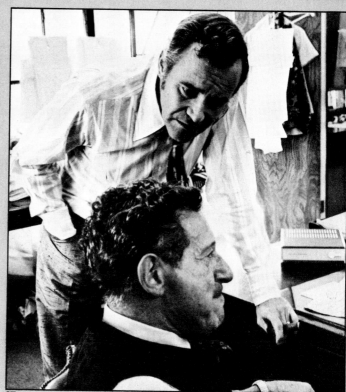

67

JALEM PRODUCTIONS, INC., AND FILMWAYS PRODUCTIONS, INC.

68. The Gilfords at home: Sam, Lisa, Jack, Madeline and Joe.
69. With Lou Jacobi in The Sunshine Boys.
70. Jack and Milton Berle, 1976, *backstage when they were "The Sunshine Boys."*

71

71. With Isaac Stern in Paris
discussing the perfect
place for nourishment.
72. During the filming of
Rhinoceros in 1972.
73. Unknown Leonardo.
74. The New Complete
Walker.
75. Living with Plants.
*From a Paperback
Booksmith catalog.*

72

BRYAN HITCHCOCK FOR PAPERBACK BOOKSMITH

73

74

75

76

76. *Madeline and Jack with Maureen Stapleton.*
77. *In* Student Prince, *1976.*
78 through 82. Making up for Sly Fox, *1977.*

77

79

80

82

81

83

83. *Portrait of the
    artist as an
    old man.*
84. *In the
    preview of*
    Merchant,
    1977.

84

COURTESY OF ITC ENTERTAINMENT, INC.
SAM THE EAGLE, COPYRIGHT © HENSEN ASSOCIATES, INC. 1976, 1978

86

85. *In Toronto on a* Fiddler *tour.*
86. *About to knock out a*
Muppet *in May 1977.*
87. *As King Henry on*
The Muppet
Show.

85

87

NEW YORK POST PHOTOGRAPH BY SHIBLA.
© 1976, NEW YORK POST CORPORATION.

★★★

he knew people who were getting rich selling home-brewed whiskey. That got my mother's full attention. Many fine points were discussed. Barrels, space, stirring techniques and the proper way to cook such a fermentation. They might have been two housewives discussing the best way to make a noodle pudding.

"They talked about what kind of pot you would use to cook this mash. (The recipe began: Take 100 pounds of prunes . . .) Where would one buy the ingredients in such large quantities? How could it be done without arousing the suspicions of the neighbors? Not to mention the cops?

"It was decided that a still could be built by a friendly plumber. It would have to fit on my mother's four-burner stove. As for the sugar, potatoes and prunes, they could be bought in five-pound quantities from various grocers by a little army of consumers enlisted by my mother.

"I'll never forget the initial purchase of those items. It was truly a mass buy. In those days, of course, foods were not prepackaged. Almost everything had to be weighed and wrapped on the spot. Potatoes were probably the only thing you'd buy in five-pound bags.

"All the cousins, uncles, aunts and in-laws, and even a few trusted friends, descended on the local grocery stores and literally stripped their shelves of those items. They worked like ants at the height of their buying season. It was probably the greatest hand operation since Pharaoh built the Pyramids with his slaves' bare hands.

" 'Leave it to Susska' was a well-worn saying in our family, and our helpers had so much confidence in my mother's schemes that they financed the purchases out of their own pockets. It didn't seem like much of a risk to them—especially after she pointed out that if she never sold any of the product she was planning to manufacture she could always repay the investors with fresh whiskey for their weddings, bar mitzvahs or late Sunday breakfasts.

"The still was ordered from the plumber, who, it turned out, had been getting inquiries from customers looking for some 'reliable' whiskey. They were mostly family people who liked a schnapps before supper. Naturally, they were also interested in not losing their eyesight after supper. My mother assured the plumber that if he made a reliable still, she'd make a reliable whiskey.

"The mash was not made as easily as the still. Experimenting was required. We began with the presser's recipe, which went on from the 100 pounds of prunes to 'place into 100-gallon barrel . . . add sugar, water to cover . . . stir, let stand for a few days . . . cover lightly . . . take a peek . . . stir . . . It should start to bubble after a few days . . . stir . . . peek . . . bubble . . .'

"The barrel was installed in a bedroom. When the bubbling first started, it sounded like a bathtub full of popcorn popping. As it gained a will of its own, it sounded like a giant pan of bacon sizzling angrily. This went on for a day and a night. Then the mixture was reaching the top of the barrel. Then it was seeping past the cover and trickling down the sides. The mop and pail were alerted and stationed at the barrel. The next day it literally cascaded over the entire bedroom floor and was heading toward the living room. Had it been liquid it would have measured a quarter of an inch deep, but it was froth and easily reached the six-inch mark. There we were, fighting to stem the bubbling tide that threatened to engulf us. The presser had told us how to start the bubbles, but as in the story 'Little Pot Boil' he'd neglected to tell us how to turn them off.

"We finally scooped up several pailfuls and that seemed to calm the angry tide. After a few more fitful starts, we learned more about quantities, techniques and for heaven's sake not too much stirring.

"About a week later we noticed a sour smell, which for me became closely associated with all my early years. I use 'associated' in its lightest sense. In a greater sense, I would say that the smell became inextricably woven into the warp and woof of our lives. It penetrated our clothes, hair, skin, and the walls and furniture in our house. People at school, on trolleys and in other tight places seemed to notice it, too. But to my knowledge no one ever got drunk from brushing up against me, and I don't remember anyone ordering a chaser when he shook hands with me. And no one was ever hopelessly addicted to me. However, for twelve years the aroma of those bubbles always hung in the air of that apartment. To this day every alcoholic drink I imbibe wakens a pinpoint memory filed away deep within my unconscious. It runs like a movie for just a few frames, a little less than a reel. 'Remember the mash, remember the mash,' it says.

"During the brewing the regular entrance to our apartment was not used. We had to enter through a side door and all the shades were drawn and we walked on tiptoe. Any unscheduled knock on the door brought a moment of terror, but miraculously no one ever surprised us on any of these cook-ins.

"Later, when my mother expanded the business and was given equal partnership in a larger operation, away from home, she did encounter some surprises that caused us more than a few minutes of agony. One day she was late getting home. Just as we were getting seriously worried, she called us (we were one of the few families in our community to have a phone) and said very calmly, 'Look, I've been caught but you are not to worry. Someone is coming to get me out of jail. Just turn the gas a little lower under the soup. I'll be home soon.' And she was home in time to serve the soup.

"Bootlegging was not, in fact, her only talent. Once, she was visiting an aunt who went into premature labor. My mother delivered the baby with such neatness and dispatch that the doctor hired her as his nurse for such at-home deliveries. She assisted him for several years. Of course, she was completely untrained and had no certification, but the doctor insisted she had natural nursing talent. So she installed that phone and bought a few white uniforms, a dark cape, a bottle of Johnson & Johnson liquid green soap and a black leather doctor's bag.

"That bag, when not in use on mercy missions, was to us what the Brinks armored trucks are to the bank. It was exactly the size of a one-gallon bottle of whiskey. The trouble was, it was too exact. The one-gallon bottle hidden in the bag made it look like a one-gallon leather bottle. A bulging, gurgling one. I never got too close to a policeman or what looked like a detective. I'm not sure which was louder, my heart or the gurgling, as I made my rounds delivering my mother's orders. To this day, I am proud to say I have a perfect record. I was never caught. My younger brother once dropped the full bag on a sidewalk in a strange neighborhood. There was nothing he could do about it. He just looked at the bag bleeding on the sidewalk and walked away.

"One of our most regular customers in Brooklyn was a maker of organs, calliopes and music rolls. He could afford more expensive whiskey than ours, but he preferred my mother's product. True to her word to the plumber, she had made a strong, fresh, nonpoisonous whiskey. It was amber (caramel coloring added), had no label and sold for a reasonable $8 a gallon. Our big customer occupied a small house in a section of mostly tenement houses. One entire loft floor was used for testing the music rolls. This went on continuously. He also had a dog with a very large bark. I suppose the competition of the music developed the dog's bark into the loudest noise I ever heard from a domestic animal.

"When my mother brought a gallon, she would knock on the downstairs door. The dog would be trying to drown out the music. My mother would call. It usually took ten minutes to attract some-one's attention upstairs. One of them would finally yell above the tumult, 'Who's there?' My mother would yell back, 'The lady from

Williamsburg.' Then the customer would let her in, saying, 'Oh, hello, the lady from Williamsburg.' He never knew her name, but the system seemed infallible because even when I would make a delivery, the same music, barking, yelling back and forth, quiet . . . they'd ask, 'Who?' I'd answer, 'I'm from the lady from Williamsburg.' "

Jack Gilford was just a little kid when he discovered that he could imitate the way a person walked or held their head to one side or smiled in a particular way. He was the kind of little kid who, if you went to his family's house, would be called in and his mother would say, "Jack, show them how Uncle Julius smokes a cigarette." He was a born mimic, though at first he wasn't terrific at voices. He got his early material from silent movies because his family was too poor to afford a radio. It wasn't until years later that he began to work on voices.

As a teenager Jack began to enter the amateur contests at movie houses around the city and also began to realize that he wanted to go into show business. To support himself while waiting to be discovered, he worked as manager of a store which sold cut-rate cosmetics. He got the high-level job by being the only employee willing to get up early enough to open the store.

One day—this is one of those success stories, remember— who should come into the store but Milton Berle, who was appearing at the Loew's Valencia around the corner. Of course, Jack recognized him. With Berle, as always, was his mother. Sadie Berle had been a department store detective before she discovered that her son Milton had a gift for acting. She was one of the most dedicated mothers in the history of show business. She breathed success into Berle. Not only did she travel with her son—whose show business work supported their entire family—but she rehearsed the orchestra while Miltie got the rest a growing boy needed and she hung the scenery to make sure it was perfect. Then she sat in the audience during every single one of Milton's performances. And to be certain of getting a seat she hired a boy named Mickey to sit through the movie and save her place. Her infectious laugh would set the audience off in a minute.

Later, when he was a grown man, Berle had to gently push Sadie away, but at this time she was—sometimes literally—pushing him onto the stage. If he was nervous, she would simply get behind him and push.

When the Berles came into the store, Jack got up all his courage and did several of his best imitations for them. He was tempted to do his Harry Langdon act, but that required a felt hat and the only hat in the store was on Berle's head. So he did Laurel and Hardy and a few other things, and then wangled an audition with Berle.

Jack Gilford was calling himself Jack Gellman then, for the simple reason that it was his real name. Berle wanted Jack to work with him, but he hated the name Gellman. Not theatrical enough, he said. Translation: Too Jewish. In those days, as I've said, you didn't want to sound too Jewish. He himself was lucky enough to have that good old Anglo-Saxon name, Milton Berle.

So he suggested a lot of colorful names like Black, Brown, Green. The only one he left out was Yellow, which would have been appropriate because Jack says he was a devout coward about going onstage even though it was what he wanted to do most of all. Jack hated every one of the names Berle proposed. He didn't much like Guilford, either, which was another Berle idea. But when he told him so, Berle said, "Okay, kid, forget it." You know how, when you're drowning, your past is supposed to flash before your eyes? Jack saw his whole future going by, before it had even happened. So he said, "Okay, I'll be Jack Guilford. But without the 'u.'" Jack's still fighting to keep that "u" out of his name. He once wrote columnist

Earl Wilson: "Dear Mr. Wuilson, please take back your 'u.'"

Jack was soon enrolled in what he calls "The Milton Berle School of Acting." He and Miltie (with Sadie and Mickey along, of course) played four shows a day and five on weekends in movie houses, and three a night in clubs all over the country.

Before he left on the tour, Jack had appeared at Brooklyn's glamorous RKO Albee Theatre in an amateur competition where he won first prize. The silver cup was presented by Abe Lyman, the orchestra leader, who invited Jack to appear at a night club in Manhattan called The Hollywood Restaurant. It was Jack's first club appearance, and Uncle Miltie gave him the first of many bits of advice.

"When you're through," he said, "let the audience applaud, take your bow and get off the stage and don't come back. You get that?" Berle had a way of repeating everything several times. "Get off the stage and don't come back," he said. He told Jack to do his imitations of Rudy Vallee, of Laurel and Hardy, and of Charles Butterworth and Al Jolson. "Do Jimmy Walker, too, and finish with the Georgie Jessel. Then get off."

Jack did what he was told, but as he was going off a tough-looking man in the wings said to him, "Hey, kid. Go back on." He looked so authoritative that Jack turned around and went back on. The thunderous ovation he had received was not repeated. He got a drizzle of applause, an anticlimax, and sat down. Jack says if he had followed Berle's advice, that audience might still be applauding today.

Another time, he and Berle were appearing in a sketch in which Jack played the part of a barker in front of a movie palace. While Berle was delivering a line, Jack absent-mindedly scratched his face. Berle immediately grabbed his hand. Afterwards, Jack asked him if he'd done anything wrong.

"Wrong?" Berle said. "You were trying to steal that scene.

Now listen, if anyone ever does that to you, correct him right onstage. Don't let him get away with it."

Jack remembered that lesson years later when as Dr. Dussel in *The Diary of Anne Frank* he was onstage with Joseph Schildkraut. The scene took place on a darkened stage in Anne's bedroom. Jack was roused from sleep by Anne's scream, and as he rushed across the stage to quiet her, Schildkraut, who was supposed to be standing by a window, was right in Jack's spot. Jack simply squeezed in front of him, edging Schildkraut back. Later, Schildkraut apologized. He claimed he'd been so excited by the scene that he just forgot himself. Which is odd, because by then he'd played it for months.

Berle also taught Jack—a boy from Williamsburg who hadn't gotten around much—how to eat chili con carne and other exotic foods. He introduced him to Barney Ross, the prizefighter, and to the world of Chicago night clubs.

Berle's style of comedy consisted mostly of one-liners and depended on perfect timing. Jack once kept count of the number of laughs Berle got: one every five seconds. But this was not the kind of comedy that appealed to Jack. He was more interested in expanding some of his mimicry into routines that had a "point." Now many comedians work this way, but Jack was one of the earliest.

After two and a half years, Jack and Berle went their separate ways, though they're still close friends and often work together. In 1976 they were teamed as The Sunshine Boys in the Arlington Park Theatre near Chicago, and they've worked on several television shows together. Every once in a while when Jack's in a play a call will come backstage for a Mr. Gellman, and Jack will know it's Berle paying him a visit. Once Berle walked through Sardi's paging Mr. Gellman.

A footnote about Mickey, the boy seat-warmer. After he stopped saving seats for Sadie Berle, Mickey went to Chicago. There the comedian Joe E. Lewis gave him a job as press agent at a night club. He even taught him how to do the job. In gratitude, Mickey gave Joe a song called "Sam, You Made the Pants Too Long." Lewis made the song famous; it became one of his trademarks. Not generally known is that "Sam, You Made the Pants Too Long" was a parody of the song "Lord, You Made the Night Too Long." The parody was written by Milton Berle for the wedding of a friend named Sam, who was a tailor. Among its most memorable lines were:

> You made the coat and vest, they fit the best,
> My fly is where my tie belongs.
> But Sam, you made the pants too long.

Years later at the Copacabana Jack heard Joe E. Lewis come out and say, "Ladies and gentlemen. Tonight I'm going to sing 'Sam, You Made the Pants Too Long,' but I'm wearing these earmuffs because I'll be goddamned if I'm going to listen to it again."

After his time with Milton Berle, Jack began to play in night clubs and vaudeville on his own and toured the Borscht Circuit. Then, in the fall of 1938, he did a benefit for the Theatre Arts Committee to aid Spain and China. The performance took place in a little club in New York called Chez Firehouse, a real firehouse converted into a beer and pretzels night club with sawdust on the floor. Jack did a few of the routines he'd worked up in the mountains. Someone from the Shubert organization was in the audience and asked Jack to audition for a new show called *Hellzapoppin.* At just about the same time a guy named Barney Josephson asked Jack to appear at a night club he was opening soon in Sheridan Square. Jack auditioned for *Hellzapoppin* but didn't get the job, so he called Barney and went to work at Cafe Society.

Cafe Society was unique. Barney wanted to own a club where blacks and whites could work together as entertainers and a mixed audience could sit out front together to watch the show. In those days there wasn't a club below 125th Street where that sort of fraternizing could go on. In fact, at the Cotton Club and other fancy Harlem rooms, whites who came to see entertainers like Duke Ellington or Ella Fitzgerald got preferred treatment and better seats than blacks.

Barney's friend John Hammond, the jazz impressario, helped him get the best jazz musicians around at the time. When Jack opened on the club's first night, December 18, 1938, the bill included Meade "Lux" Lewis, Albert Ammons, Pete Johnson playing six-handed boogie-woogie piano, and Joe Turner, the blues shouter. Eventually there were some girl singers, among them Billie Holiday and a beautiful lady named Helena Horne. (Barney got her to change her name to Helena because he didn't like Lena; later, she changed it back.)

Jack was the M.C., the only white person on the bill. It was in the depths of the Depression, but on opening night Cafe Society was jammed all the way to the little dance floor. Josephson had engaged some of Zero's WPA artist friends, like Adolf Dehn, Gregor Duncan, Refregier, William Gropper and Abe Birnbaum, to decorate the place with murals. Actually, he didn't pay them in cash; they got due bills for food and drink at the club.

Barney called Jack into his office and said that while everything else had been arranged, the cabaret license hadn't come through yet so would he please not get any laughs. People could drink and dance and listen to music, but they were not supposed to be "entertained." These may have been the strangest directions a comedian ever got. Of course, Jack couldn't help himself. He went out on the stage and did his movie routine, in which he gave quick capsule summaries of various kinds of movies, with a description of a Grade B mystery where the first scene has a castle on a hill, the moon scudding behind the clouds, and when the hero knocks on the door the butler opens it. And, Jack said, "We all knew then that The Butler Did It." The line has become part of the language and Jack invented it. That opening-night audience laughed. Barney failed to report the fact that illegal entertaining had gone on at his place, and ten years later, when he lost his license, they mentioned that evening's transgression. But by then Barney's place had become known as a "radical hotbed" where "leftists" came to see people like Zero and Jack perform. It certainly sounds as though politics, not Jack's jokes, got the license revoked.

Jack dressed "back to back" with Billie Holiday in Cafe Society's only dressing room. One night Billie sang "Strange Fruit," Abe Meerepol's song that had first been presented in *Pens and Pencils*. When her mother heard it, she asked Billie, "Why do you want to stick your neck out by singing that song?"

Billie responded, "Listen, I'm proud to be singing an anti-lynching song. Someday there'll be a better world for our people."

"Perhaps," said her mother, "but you won't live to see it."

"Maybe not," said Billie, "but when it happens I'm going to be dancing in my grave."

Billie Holiday's boyfriend was her accompanist at Cafe Society, and one day Barney caught him smoking what in those days we called "tea." Barney fired him, and on the piano player's last night Billie decided to try to save his job. It was three in the morning, the place was empty and Barney was standing in the doorway ready to go home. The lights were all out except for a smoky spot above the piano. The piano player sat down at the keyboard, and Billie, looking directly at Barney, sang "Lover Man." It was a touching moment, but Barney was not moved. The piano player left the next day. Billie followed soon after.

Barney told Jack that he could stay at Cafe Society forever —which turned out to be two weeks. When Barney said he'd have to leave, Jack asked, "So what happened to forever?"

Barney Josephson hadn't always been a night club operator. He started out as a shoestore buyer with a crazy dream about opening a new kind of night club. But he always took the advice of the last person he spoke to. Most of the time they were smart people with imagination—people like John Hammond, who encouraged him to have Josh White and Susan Reed and other folk singers in a night club even if it had never been done before. But at this particular moment someone had told him that he had to change the show every two weeks.

Jack could understand the reasoning. He'd come from vaudeville, where shows changed all the time because the same people came to the theater every week. So he got another job. He was booked into the Hotel Roosevelt in New Orleans with Shep Fields and his Rippling Rhythm. Then Barney changed his mind, but Jack was committed so he tried to get as a replacement a young entertainer named Danny Kaye whom he'd met in the mountains that summer. Danny said he didn't have an act or enough material to work one up at such short notice. (That was BSF—Before Sylvia Fine, his talented wife, who later wrote almost all of his special material.)

Jack went to New Orleans, then returned to Cafe Society, where the policy had changed and the show remained about the same for eight months until Billie Holiday left. Afterwards, it seemed to Jack that the acts were a little heavy on the masculine side. There were three fat boogie-woogie piano players, one tall black blues singer and one curly-headed Jewish M.C. "You've got to get a girl," Jack said. "You can't have a night club show without a girl entertainer." Barney said he knew that, but he didn't like any of the girls the agent had been sending him—they were all torch singers, complete with long chiffon handkerchiefs. Jack thought a minute and then said, "Hey, why don't you get that girl pianist who used to sit in with the band? Remember her? Hazel Scott." So Hazel Scott and Jack were on the same bill together. This episode and the next illustrate that there are only 200 people in the world. They all know each other. Everyone else has been sent here by Central Casting to fill in the empty spaces.

One day, many years after Jack had left Cafe Society, Barney called and said, "Listen, I have this new comedian, a young fellow, a fat funny fellow. He's a painter, actually, but he was recommended by Ivan Black, my press agent. His name is Sam Mostel. Why don't you come down and look at him and tell me what you think?" Jack went down on a night when there was a very sparse audience. He remembers a "round fellow, a little crazy, but funny" who went on and performed. Barney asked Jack what he thought, and Jack said, "Well, he's certainly funny, but his numbers run a little too long." Barney thanked him and introduced Sam Mostel, soon to be Zero. Jack remembers that Zero did a peculiar little ballet–boogie-woogie while they were shaking hands, but Zero always vigorously denied this. He claimed he'd never mix dances like that.

Cafe Society became THE place to go—for everyone from Mrs. Roosevelt to Bob Hope. Though it specialized in jazz, the club featured a mix of topical satirical humor and good music in a friendly atmosphere—the kind of entertainment provided much later at The Hungry i in San Francisco and Second City in Chicago.

Despite all the action, though, Barney was going broke. His solution was to replace the old Cafe with a new one uptown on Fifty-eighth Street. Instead of announcing the closing of the downtown Cafe, Ivan Black put out the word that Barney was expanding, that business was so good downtown he was opening another place to take the spillover. That did it. Pretty soon, both places were jumping. Cafe Society Uptown opened October 8, 1940. The menu for opening night included celery, olives, shrimps, oysters and clams, a couple of soups, a two-inch prime filet mignon with mushrooms, two vegetables, a choice of potatoes and dessert. The price for the meal was $1.50.

One night, while he was still working for Barney, the others on the bill were off doing a benefit somewhere and Jack had to do the two o'clock show alone. He played his regular M.C. role, saying, "I'd like to introduce Albert Ammons. But Albert Ammons isn't here." Jack then played all the parts, pantomiming Ammons at the piano and even pretending to be Billie Holiday. It was hilarious. A film producer who saw that off-the-cuff performance told Jack he ought to be in a show called *Meet the People,* which was running in Hollywood and would eventually come to Broadway.

Jack made plans to go to the Coast immediately. He was so anxious to get into a Broadway cast that he didn't give a second thought to leaving his job and going on a long, expensive trip, all the way across the country, to do it. He wasn't even discouraged when, a few nights later, the same producer showed up and, on seeing Jack's train ticket, said, "My God, I don't remember anything about it! I must have been drunk."

Jack set off anyhow on the polar route to Broadway, but when he got to Hollywood the *Meet the People* people didn't want to meet him. He couldn't even get an audition. He did, however, get invited to a party where he was asked to entertain, and Elliott Sullivan, who just happened to be in *Meet the People,* just happened to be in the room. "Hey," he said, "are you by any chance interested in joining our show?"

On December 25, 1940, *Meet the People* opened in New York, exactly one year after its Los Angeles opening. Unfortunately, on the same night a little show called *Pal Joey* also opened, and guess what show the first-string critics went to? Still, *Meet the People* had a fair run, and Jack Gilford's theatrical career was launched. He was now less than sure of his future, though, and he was afraid the Broadway theater he was appearing in might soon be torn down for a parking lot. So he moonlighted at Cafe Society Uptown, occasionally taking Lena Horne home after work (they both lived in Brooklyn).

★★

At about this time, the war caught up with him and he was drafted—only to be turned down at his medical exam. They said it was because he was in psychotherapy (which was practically a hanging offense, instead of the sign of social status it is today). Jack feels that they simply wanted very much to win the war. As the joke of the day went, "When they take me, the Japs will be in the lobby."

Instead, Jack enlisted in the USO and was sent to the Pacific, where he traveled around with a motley band of entertainers consisting of an accordion player, an attractive female dancer, two girl comedy acrobats and a 235-pound blond girl singer with so much personality that every soldier was in love with her by the time she got to the microphone.

The accordion player was nearly blind, but he was a very proud man who didn't want any help. He simply followed Jack around, letting Jack lead him in a casual sort of way. In order to help the fellow out, Jack had to walk very slowly, and he soon found that his whole life was slowing up—his legs, his pulse, his breathing—all to accommodate the accordion player.

For the three months they were stationed in Honolulu, there were peace rumors. Then one night, when they were entertaining at Pearl Harbor, there was a great roar from the crowd in the middle of the singer's act. An officer immediately came onstage and told the soldiers to be quiet and show a little respect, but Jack stepped forward and said, "I've been in show business a long time, but no one ever told me what to do if war ended in the middle of a show. I think we should all just yell our heads off."

The war was over. Madeline and Mitchell were living in Manhattan. Jack was back at Cafe Society Downtown, working in night clubs and summering in the Borscht Belt. And Zero and I, newly married, were living in Manhattan. Like everyone else after the war, we were ready to get on with it. None of us realized that the magic days were over and the bad times were about to begin.

•　　　•　　　•

Zero and I found an apartment on Forty-sixth Street between Fifth and Sixth avenues in a building owned by a big celebrity.
One of the previous tenants had been Moss Hart, and Zero and I
thought maybe some of their theatrical luck would rub off on us.

The apartment was built on three levels and the elevator
opened right into our front hall. The living room had leaded glass
windows across the entire front and a window seat. There were
skylights with twelve leaded glass windows in both the living room
and the bedroom. And the same leaded glass windows were in the
bathroom and in the dinette. Sounds beautiful, doesn't it?

It *was* beautiful on a lovely clear day when you couldn't tell
that every one of those lovely leaded glass panes was warped. That
was only obvious when it rained. Then water poured into the apartment, and the wind blew through the place like the mistral in the
South of France. The heat wasn't like in the South of France,
though. In fact, there was very little of it at any time, and for what
there was we were at the mercy of the superintendent, a gentleman
seriously devoted to drinking. When he was on duty, he brought our
guests up in the elevator, but after six o'clock we'd have to go down
and get them. They'd ride in splendor in our fancy private car and
step into our freezing apartment hoping that the warmth of our
hospitality would eventually thaw them out.

The climate resulted in our creating some strange at-home
costumes. Early-morning dishabille for me consisted of a flannel
nightgown, bathrobe and a red flannel shirt of Zero's. On my dainty
feet and legs were a pair of Zero's knee socks. The man of the house
was similarly attired, except that his costume was topped off with a
helmet liner. He was bald, you remember, so his head got cold.

Our two winters in that apartment were spent in a search for
warmth. We had a fireplace, but anything you could burn either cost
a lot of money or was scarce. My closest friends in those days were

the guys on Canal Street who ran the coal and log outlet stores. To this day, whenever I look for a new apartment I first investigate the heat, and after that I look at the closets.

We did great business in that apartment in spite of the weather conditions. Because of our central location, people would drop in on the way to the theater and come back for a little after-theater snort and snack on the way home. We were Sardi's strongest competition for a while.

Once, a radio actor we knew heard another actor say to the director of the show, "I have a date for the theater tonight, but I don't know where to take her afterwards."

"Take her to Zero's," the director directed.

"I don't even know Zero," the actor said.

"But he'll be hurt if you don't come," said the director.

Another day Sam Jaffe ran into an actor he knew standing on a street corner with his bags. He had just been discharged from the army and had been trying in vain to get a hotel room. Sam was equal to the occasion: "Go to Zero's. He's just around the corner," he suggested. So we gained a boarder. The guy slept in our dinette for eight months. Every time we heard about an available apartment, we'd tell him about it. "Oh, I've seen it," he'd say. "I wouldn't live there." Of course not. There he'd have to pay.

By the time he'd been with us about half a year I got tired of dragging Zero into the bathroom whenever I wanted to have a fight with him. So, periodically I would say to Zero, "He's your friend, you tell him to leave." And he'd say, "Okay, I will. Tomorrow." But he never did. One day while I was pregnant and Zero was out of town, I just asked our boarder to go. And, by golly, he went. It was that simple.

We saw a lot of Phil Loeb when we lived on Forty-sixth Street because he lived nearby. One time when he was at our house an actor called him to read him a speech. Phil was on the bedroom phone while Zero listened on the phone downstairs. As usual, I was engaged in trying to keep the place warm by putting another $10 log on the fire. Suddenly, a spark flew out of the fireplace onto a lantern filled with kerosene. The lantern flared up and a chair burst into flames. Zero dropped the phone and picked up the first thing he saw to smother the fire: Phil's coat.

We were making so much noise that Phil came downstairs and yelled, "What the hell are you doing with my new coat?" We explained, he was placated and then he remembered the actor on the phone. He ran to pick up the receiver and, do you know, that guy was still going on? Even deadpan Phil laughed.

During the war, when meat was rationed and only people who bought it on the black market had as much as they wanted, Zero was asked to entertain for the butcher's union. As part payment they sent over a huge rib roast, a species we hadn't seen for years. Zero had one simple principle about eating: no leftovers. So we had to find some deserving person to help us eat the roast.

We crossed off Sam Jaffe because of his being a vegetarian. Em and Lou Paley were in the country and no one else seemed deserving enough. It looked like we'd have to eat six pounds of meat by ourselves until as I was taking the roast out of the oven, I thought: Phil. I called him and said, "Listen, if you want some roast beef, come over immediately. Don't bother to change."

In a few minutes the bell rang. Z went down in our private elevator, and when he opened the door there stood Phil. Stark naked. "You said come as you are," he said. (Thankfully, he'd put a raincoat over his bare body for the trip over and had brought some clothes along to put on while he ate.)

Another time, when Phil was at a party at our place, it got very late and we invited him to spend the night on our couch. He protested that he wouldn't think of disturbing us in that way—he only lived around the corner and could walk home in a minute. After about fifteen minutes of protestations, he finally said, "All right, if you insist," and, right there, he began to peel off his clothes until there he stood—in his pajamas.

One freezing morning while we were lounging around in our usual bizarre attire, we heard the elevator coming up. As usual, the door opened right in our apartment, but this time it wasn't a practical jokester or any indigent actor—this time two FBI men came into our lives.

It turned out they were there to ask Zero some questions about a high school classmate. Zero hardly knew the guy, and we figured they'd just come up to case us and the apartment. I'd love to have seen their report on what the well-known actor and his elegant wife looked like. We looked like those people who sleep under the bridges in Paris, that's who.

After they asked their questions and were preparing to leave, I said to them, "Listen, you guys get around a lot. If you hear of an apartment, would you let us know?" They smiled and said, "Sure," but you couldn't trust them. They never came up with even a cold-water flat.

All of this took place while we were still innocent, before we knew that you didn't have to let the FBI into your house and you certainly didn't have to talk to them. In the years that followed we learned more than we wanted to about those things. That visit to our freezing little place on Forty-sixth Street was the beginning of a time that shouldn't happen to a shanty Irish girl from Philadelphia.

6

★★★

BLACKLIST

It's hard for me to tell about the blacklist. We've kept those memories buried for so long that it's rough to dredge them up.

We were lucky. No one close to us was an informer. People we were acquainted with informed—even people Zero worked with —but no bosom friend caved in. It was really rough on the people whose close friends were friendly witnesses.

I'm sure you remember John Garfield, even if only from *The Late Show*. In the 1940's he was one of Warner Brothers' top stars. His first big hit was *Four Daughters*, and then he did *Destination Tokyo, Body and Soul* and *Gentlemen's Agreement.* He was a darling friend and we loved him. (Years later, his daughter Julie played the role of Zero's daughter in *The Merchant*, his last play.)

John Garfield's background was in the Group Theatre, founded by Lee Strasberg, Harold Clurman and Cheryl Crawford. The playwright who was mostly associated with the Group was Clifford Odets, the author of *Golden Boy, Awake and Sing* and *Rocket to the Moon.* Elia "Gadge" Kazan was an actor-director who started with the Group and then went on to do movies and Broadway plays. Gadge and Clifford Odets were both brilliant and—everyone thought—honorable men. So we were all shocked when they were friendly witnesses.

Especially hard-hit was John Garfield, who was not an "intellectual," but a warm, lovely, talented actor who had looked up to Clifford and Gadge Kazan as the big thinkers of the group. When Garfield was called before the House Un-American Activities Committee, he didn't want to cooperate, so he couldn't understand why both Clifford and Gadge in one month were both friendly witnesses. John was being pulled one way by Warners and another by his principles. And he couldn't survive. He died of a heart attack.

Clifford Odets was at his funeral, and at the Garfield house, after we came home from the cemetery, he sat defending the position he had taken before the Committee. He said there were several things he felt had to be said to the Committee, and the only way he could say them was if he cooperated, because the rule was if you answered any question except your name and address, and then refused to answer any other question, you could be held in contempt of Congress. The only way to avoid contempt was to refuse to answer anything on the grounds of the Fifth Amendment.

Clifford said that he had really told the Committee off, that his having given names was immaterial (Maestro, play "Hearts and Flowers") and that he couldn't be judged by anyone who hadn't read all of his testimony, not just that part quoted in *The New York Times.* Alfred Crown, a movie producer friend of Garfield's, said, "You could have taken an ad. I would have paid."

I don't want to go over old ground when I speak about the blacklist. God knows there's been a lot of blacklist talk over the years. Zero's film *The Front* describes one aspect; books, articles and even dissertations are being written about it every day. (We would qualify for a blacklist Ph.D. if they gave them for experience.)

When we remember the blacklist, what we talk about is a

little different: political, sure, but remember we were family people —mamas and papas who happened to be in the theater but who had to feed their kids. Some of what happened to us seems funny now. But not much. A lot of it seems insane, like *Alice in Wonderland* with the FBI and HUAC playing the roles of the Mad Hatter and the March Hare.

The other side didn't always know what to make of us, either. I always wonder what they thought that cold winter day in 1954 when the FBI followed Madeline into Washington Square Park. It was their regular first Tuesday of the month—Madeline Gilford Surveillence Day—and the fact that she was so pregnant she couldn't bend over to tie her shoelaces, let alone overthrow a government, didn't deter them. They kept an eagle eye on her anyway.

Madeline was pushing Joe in his carriage, with Lisa holding on to the other hand, when from newspaper pictures she'd seen she recognized Alger Hiss standing across the park. It was Alger's first day out of jail, and Madeline went up to him and said, "You don't know me, but I want to welcome you back to the Village and tell you how much we admire you." Out of the corner of her eye she saw the poor FBI men dressed in their thin raincoats, clutching their regulation snap-brim fedoras in the wind, and she decided to give them a little show. As they watched, open-mouthed, Madeline gave Alger Hiss a welcome-home kiss. And then she led her little group of children and dutiful federal cops into the supermarket.

Years later, Alger Hiss told Edelaine Harburg that the nicest thing that happened to him on his first day out of jail was that a pregnant lady had come up to him and kissed him.

Zero had a favorite blacklist encounter, too. He was walking on Fifth Avenue when he ran into an old actor friend. They stood for a moment or two talking about the usual things, like the weather and families.

Then the actor asked Zero: "Are you working?"

Z answered, "No, I'm not working."

"Well," said the actor, "I know why you're not working; you're blacklisted. But why the hell ain't I working?"

Zero did have some work now and then, courtesy of some old friends. For instance, in 1950 Elia Kazan hired him to do his first serious role, the villain in a movie called *Panic in the Streets.* The film was shot in New Orleans, and after it was finished Kazan persuaded Darryl Zanuck, head of Twentieth Century–Fox, to give Zero a bonus of nine weeks' salary.

Later, Z got minor roles in pictures like *The Enforcers* and *Sirocco* with Humphrey Bogart at Warner's, and other small jobs at Twentieth. But no one was more surprised than I when during this period he was asked to sign a seven-year contract with Fox. It meant that we'd have to move from New York, put all our things in storage and prepare to stay in Los Angeles for one year, minimum. But the contract sounded like heaven, so we sent the clothes and books and records by truck, gave up our wonderful, cheap apartment and took off.

In Los Angeles we rented a regulation movie colony type house with a swimming pool. One day, as we were sitting by the pool, the water began to slosh about alarmingly, setting up a minia-ture tidal wave. As the water rose to where we were sitting, Zero turned to me and said, "Well, Kate, looks like you got another lemon." Though that particular California earthquake was not en-tirely my fault, from then on anytime something went wrong Z would say, "Well, Kate, another lemon."

What we didn't really understand was that when they say one-year contract in Hollywood it doesn't really mean twelve months' work. What it means is that the studio has to pay you for thirty-six weeks. The rest of the year there's no guarantee of a salary.

And naturally, with the way things were going, that's what happened to us. When we got there, Zero worked six weeks on *Mr.*

Belvedere Rings the Bell and then was put on layoff. So, even before our clothes got to the West Coast, he had to go back to the East Coast to earn money to keep us in Hollywood.

There was a long spell of silence from the studio and he wasn't assigned to any more pictures, so, ever alert, we figured the blacklist had finally hit Hollywood. Later, when Zero was called before HUAC and they asked him if he had been in Hollywood or the State of California after 1942 "for the purposes of carrying on his profession," he answered, "Oh yes, I was . . . I was signed to a contract with Twentieth Century–Fox . . . or was it Eighteenth Century–Fox?" The chairman objected to this slur on one of America's most prominent film companies, so Zero amended it to "Nineteenth Century–Fox." He had compromised, but they deleted that from the record of his hearing. And when Zero pointed at the Committee chairman and, in a loud stage whisper, said, "That man is a schmuck," they deleted that, too. Later in his testimony Zero said that he failed to see what crime there was in his "imitation of a butterfly at rest." Congressman Jackson told him he shouldn't put his butterfly to rest so that it brought any money into the coffers of the Communist party, and Congressman Doyle cautioned Zero to "put the bug to rest somewhere else next time."

Very fancy discourse you got in government chambers in those days.

There we were, paupers in a town of millionaires having to sit out a year's contract with no work. Zero was lucky. He had his painting. He got a little studio for $10 a week in a building on Santa Monica Boulevard and painted the year away. Josh went to kindergarten, where on his first report card he got a B in Keeping Hands Away from Face—a subject that fascinates me. (How did they know? Did they have hidden cameras?) And I sat around and waited for a reprieve.

When his contract had about three months to go, Twentieth

Century–Fox was asked to lend Zero to Columbia Pictures for a star part in *Happy Time,* produced by Stanley Kramer. Twentieth couldn't get rid of him fast enough, though he left an indelible impression on them with such gems as *The Model and The Marriage Broker* and several other films so memorable I've never been able to find them even on late-night TV.

He signed with Columbia to do *Happy Time* and was given a starting date and a schedule of seven weeks' work, but on arrival he found he was not allowed on the set and was not going to be used. Who told him? The director? The producer? The set designer? No —he read it in the trades. When Typhoid Mary was paid off, we said, "The hell with it, we'll go home."

After the announcement that Zero had been fired appeared, Gadge Kazan called from New York. (This was before he testified before HUAC.) He said, "Don't worry, I've got a job for you here. Come on back." The job was in a play called *Flight into Egypt* by George Tabori. It was directed by Gadge and produced by Irene Selznick (Louis B. Mayer's daughter and David Selznick's ex-wife). It couldn't miss, could it? If those people didn't know a hit when they read it, who did? It was the most heralded play of the season, and the theater parties were lining up for it. We moved back to New York—to the apartment of Jules Dassin, who had already been blacklisted and was in Europe looking for work.

The play opened in New Haven, and I went up for the big event. I sat, all dressed up, for two and a half hours of torture, which is what all actors' wives feel on opening night. We've heard all the troubles, shared all the hysterics and the laughs about rehearsals. We know our husbands' parts backwards from having to cue them while they're learning the lines. We've tried desperately to think up cute, appropriate opening-night gifts for the cast. Then comes the big night, and we have nothing to do but worry. I always felt it would have been much easier if I had the lemonade concession. Then, at least, I'd keep busy, and if the show was a flop we'd have made a little something out of it anyhow.

Flight into Egypt, as you may have guessed, was a non-success. Not an instant flop that closed in four performances, but definitely not a success.

We've all had our share of flops, and none of us can tell in advance—I don't think there's an actor in the world who can—when a play is just going to bomb. For one thing, by the time you're involved in the play you've gotten too close to it. Madeline says that even if you suspect the play might not win the Pulitzer Prize, you are, after all, a person who acts for a living and a play with a role in it for you is a JOB. She's got a point. Still, it's awful when the thing's a turkey and everyone knows it but you. Movies are not so hard on us, because by the time they open we're onto something else. If you're in a bad play, you have to go to the theater every night and stand there with egg on your face.

Jack was once in a play called *The Passion of Gross.* It was at the Theatre de Lys, which is just a short walk from the Gilfords' apartment in the Village. Even though it ran only one week, he had to drag his feet over there until the thing finally closed. But there was an added problem. The play was directed by the husband of Kermit Bloomgarden's ace play reader, and so Bloomgarden came to see it. He was planning to put Jack into his next production, *The Diary of Anne Frank,* and there were a few chancy days when, having seen him in this awful play, Bloomgarden almost changed his mind about giving Jack the part. That's just another hazard of being in a bad play. It's hard to do good work in a flop. The critics said after *The Passion of Gross,* "Bring back 'Three Penny Opera.'" Ironically, when *Passion* closed, *Three Penny* did open again, and during its seven-year run Madeline got to play Mrs. Peachum for six months.

Zero had several major flops: *A Stone for Danny Fisher*

played for a big six weeks; Brecht's *Good Woman of Setzuan* only stayed open for a short time. Then in 1957, during the blacklist, Zero was called in to replace an actor in the play *Good as Gold*. This looked like a big winner. It was written by John Patrick, whose last play had been *Teahouse of the August Moon*. Cheryl Crawford was the producer. She was one of the founders of the Group Theatre. They had good taste, didn't they?

Good as Gold opened in Boston, where one critic objected to their making fun of the FBI, so it was rewritten so as not to make fun of the Bureau. It ran five days. The winner of the What-Do-You-Say-to-an-Actor-When-You-Go-Backstage award goes to Ring Lardner, who showed up in Zero's dressing room and said, with great conviction, "This is undoubtedly the WORST play I've ever seen." Don't think you can get away with that, however. It was months before I forgave him. My advice is, if you go backstage, lie like a dog. Who'll know?

Flight into Egypt closed. And suddenly there were other problems. It wasn't bad enough that we'd been involved in a theatrical disaster. We closed our show, and the House Un-American Activities Committee opened theirs in New York.

HUAC's New York hearings were not aimed at the most famous Broadway actors. HUAC was out to get a little group of stalwarts, mostly members of the American Federation of Television and Radio Artists (AFTRA), who had banded together to oppose a vociferous anti-red group calling itself AWARE, INC.

AWARE went after people who worked in broadcasting. Madeline saw an AWARE bulletin that made it clear that the AFTRA union leadership had joined in blacklisting the actors they had just defeated in a union election. The AWARE leadership, the bulletin proved, labeled anyone running against the established slate as "pro-red." This prevented those people from getting jobs and, by the way, cut down the competition in the overcrowded acting business.

Madeline was outraged and immediately became one of the leaders of those opposing AWARE. Since Sam Gilford was only ten days old at the time, Jack stayed home and baby-sat while Madeline pulled together the case. Jack couldn't get work anyhow, but he says that she was out of the house for two years during the blacklist, leaving him to do everything but nurse the baby.

To stop blacklisting, it was decided to enlist as many people from the old days of radio and television as possible. Madeline became a leader in that effort because she'd been in radio since her childhood and knew everybody. In fact, the resolution condemning AWARE was written in the Gilfords' apartment at three in the morning, with Madeline taking time off to nurse Sam during the deliberations. It passed in March, and in June, by a strange coincidence, HUAC's first subpoena was served—on our old friend Stanley Prager.

Stanley, knowing that HUAC was after him, had moved to a new apartment and taken a post office box. One day he went to pick up his mail, and there, standing near his box, was a young, handsome black man. Stanley was very active in helping black actors get roles on Broadway, so when this man said, "Stanley Prager?" Stanley answered, "Yes." And found a summons in his hand.

He immediately called Madeline, who was on Fire Island, to warn her that she would probably be next. They decided she could expect a visit momentarily from one Dolores Scotti, the investigator for HUAC who specialized in show business.

Madeline's daily Fire Island routine was simple; she'd feed, launder and dress everyone, then take her little red wagon and her three children to the grocery store and the post office for her letter from Jack, who was away working to pay for this shabby Shangri-la.

The day they tried to serve her she was on the way home, dragging her wagon containing Joe and the groceries, pushing the carriage with Sam in it and calling to Lisa over her shoulder. When she reached her little summer cottage, she lifted the groceries with one hand, pushed Joe up the steps with her knee and had just bent down to take Sam out of his carriage when she noticed a pair of black Dr. Scholl's oxfords peeping out of the bushes. Now, Fire Island is a very informal place. People don't wear Dr. Scholl's black oxfords. They don't even wear shoes. And why, thought Madeline, would a lady visitor be standing in her bushes? Unless, of course, she was Dolores Scotti. Madeline said, "Uh-oh," and began to head for the safety of the house. But Scotti was not loaded down with babies and groceries. She beat Madeline to the porch steps and said, "Madeline Lee?"

Madeline said nothing.

Scotti said, "You *are* Madeline Lee."

Madeline said, "I'm the baby-sitter. You don't know who I am."

Scotti responded, "I've seen you act."

Madeline, who hadn't acted in years and wasn't doing too good a job right then, was tempted to say, "Where, in the maternity ward?" Instead she said, "You're trespassing on private property. I command you to leave."

Scotti said, "You're Madeline Lee and I'm not leaving."

Madeline answered, "Get off these steps," and then swung swiftly around with her right arm to forcibly eject Scotti with her elbow.

In so doing she hit Dolores Scotti with Sam Gilford. The head of the six-month-old baby hit the head of the process server and sent the subpoena flying into the bushes, where Scotti must have decided to consider it served. She left on the next ferry.

It was at fund-raising parties on Fire Island that John Henry Faulk got active in the fight against AWARE, INC., and as a result got himself blacklisted.

Faulk sued. Louis Nizer, his lawyer, won a landmark libel

decision against AWARE, INC., Johnson and Hartnett. Faulk was awarded three and a half million bucks. Finally, blacklisting became too expensive for anybody. And to think it all started when Madeline hit Dolores Scotti with her six-month-old son.

See, you never know when your kids will come through for you!

Twenty-two assorted people were called before the Committee. Most of them were actors and actresses who had done a lot of work in radio or television. But there were exceptions: Susie d'Usseau was a painter, Ivan Black was Zero's old press agent from Cafe Society Downtown days. The Committee was obviously cutting a wide swath through the community.

Jack was appearing in the Midwest when a man who looked like an autograph seeker came up to him and said, "Jack Gilford?"

Jack smiled. "Yes," he said.

"I'm glad you're smiling," the man said, "because I'm about to do something unpleasant." And he served him. Leonard Patrick, producer-director of the theater, wired the Committee that he would hold them responsible for the failure of his venture if they insisted that his star come to New York for their hearing. Apparently, being accused of disrupting the free-enterprise system made the Committee feel un-American, for Jack's appearance was postponed. He finally came before the Committee in 1956, but by then the blacklist was no longer such a threat.

The New York HUAC hearings were scheduled to begin for a limited one-week run on August 14, 1955. During July those of the "Chosen" who were in New York met at Susie d'Usseau's apartment to rehearse for their appearances. Rehearsals were held around eleven-thirty at night to give Stanley Prager a chance to come from *Pajama Game*. A screenwriter and a director who had once been a lawyer were the head coaches in trying to prepare people to withstand the onslaught and pressure of the Committee's brand of tricky questioning. They used what we now call "role playing." One of them would take the part of the witness while the rest of the group would shoot questions at them.

Susie was a little hard of hearing, and questions often had to be repeated for her. Once she was asked that most famous of all questions: "Are you now or have you ever been a member of the Communist party?"

Susie replied: "Would you mind rephrasing that question?"

Later, in a similar session, when Jack was asked that other favorite question, "Do you believe in the overthrow of the United States government by force and violence?" he replied, "No, just gently."

These funny, talented people were encouraged to be themselves. If you're funny naturally, okay, be funny. If you're a big talker, that's marvelous, because the longer you stay on the stand the fewer witnesses the Committee will be able to call. The coaching also taught them how to take the Fifth Amendment. The idea was to try to state the principles of the First Amendment but to take the Fifth when it looked like you'd otherwise end up in jail.

Dolores Scotti was confident that witnesses would be cooperative, but by midweek the New York papers told of their wholesale defiance.

In fact, Madeline followed the only friendly witness onto the stand. She was devastated by his testimony and it took her a moment or two to collect herself, but once in control she gave one of the stellar performances of her career. It is in the record that Committee Member Representative Willis told his colleagues at one point in Madeline's loquacious testimony: "She will run out of words. Let her rant a little bit." He obviously had never met our girl.

Zero, for example, would listen to the first sentence of one of Madeline's stories, and, if it didn't hold much promise, he'd run

116

****

MOSTEL/GILFORD

like a thief. Her stories ramble so much, I think of her as all tributaries and no river (but with love, you understand). I've learned to use the time Madeline is talking to do aerobics to strengthen my stomach muscles. Jack . . . well, no, this is, after all, a family book, and what he does has no place here.

On the occasion of her testimony before HUAC, Madeline's love of the spoken word and her skill in stretching a sentence to its limits saved the next few witnesses from having to testify. The Committee had met its match.

The hearings were over on August 17, and on Labor Day weekend I took the children and went to Atlantic City for a peaceful weekend. Zero was in California doing *Lunatics and Lovers.* His day before the Committee came in the fall. They held a special hearing for him in California. You can imagine how grateful he was for the accommodation. We were living in a big apartment on Eighty-sixth Street at the time, and my mother, who was not well, had moved in with us. The place was $225 a month and expensive for us, so we asked Phil Loeb if he'd like to move in, too. We would charge him $60. Phil, who'd been living alone in one hotel or another for years, was glad to take up our offer.

Phil had had a rotten few years. The blacklist had not only kept him from working, it had humiliated him and beaten him down. He had a son who was seriously ill, and it cost thousands of dollars a year to keep him in a good hospital. So, under pressure from blacklisters, when Phil was offered a settlement for giving up the part of Jake on *The Goldbergs,* he accepted. And though everyone understood, Phil never forgave himself.

In addition, Phil had just had operations for cataracts, and he was terrified that he'd never be able to see well enough to work, even if the bad times would eventually be over. His peripheral vision was affected, and Phil used to say, "My talent in acting is my freedom on the stage, and if I can't see, that will go." He'd been depressed for months.

One night I came into our living room and Phil was hanging out the window, looking like he was trying to make up his mind to jump. The only way I could deal with that was by yelling at him the way a mother would yell at a naughty child. "You get back into your room," I screamed, "and don't you ever do anything like that again." Phil meekly obeyed.

But on that Labor Day weekend he was alone in our apartment. He took the subway to midtown and checked in at the Hotel Taft under the assumed name of Fred Lang. It was at the Taft that we had held most of our Equity meetings.

Whenever anyone wants to drive home the tragedy of the blacklist, they tell about how Phil Loeb committed suicide in that hotel room. He became a symbol of how bad things were.

Phil is not a symbol for us. We remember him as one of the funniest, dearest men we ever knew, our true and funny friend. To this day we find ourselves constantly telling Phil Loeb stories. He has not been replaced, and when we think of the blacklist insanity, the most insane, unforgettable and unbelievable thing is that it killed Phil Loeb.

Jack got blacklisted just as he was branching out into a new career—television.

One of the first TV variety shows was *The Phil Silvers Arrow Show,* and Jack was asked to appear during its first season. Madeline was in the living room when the phone rang, and she heard Jack turn down the job. He knew he couldn't do it, he explained. The show was going to run for twenty weeks, and he didn't have enough material for twenty weeks. Patiently, Madeline tried to explain that TV wasn't like vaudeville or night clubs. They had writers on TV.

In fact, *The Arrow Show* had lots of writers, and two of the very brightest young men were Danny and "Doc" Simon. Danny later became a director, and Doc, of course, is Neil Simon, author of *The Odd Couple, Plaza Suite, The Prisoner of Second Avenue,*

The Sunshine Boys, and we've lost track of how many other big hits.

The show ran for twenty weeks, and for the last six of these Jack was promoted to first feature billing. He was just beginning to enjoy the whole thing when they began to blacklist people like him.

The TV blacklist started with a small, badly printed book called *Red Channels,* which looked like nothing anyone would ever take seriously. Madeline and her friends at CBS sat around in a restaurant laughing about how ridiculous it was that radio's earliest and best stars were listed. The laughter didn't last long.

Soon there were no jobs in television for Jack or Phil Loeb or many others among our friends. Jack had been rehearsing with Fred Allen for Allen's TV debut in several sketches, and one included Jack's own "sleeping bit." Jack does a very realistic imitation of a man fighting to keep his eyes open and eventually, but painfully, losing the battle. He got a call from his agent at the William Morris office that the sketch had been dropped, that the producers had decided to "go another way," that they were sorry but they would pay him his fee for the performance. Jack, suspecting the blacklist, told his agent that since he was hired to do the part, he had every intention of doing it, and that he would be going to the next scheduled rehearsal. Jack's motive was not to get back the part. He knew even then that it would be impossible to do that. He just wanted to embarrass the producers. At the stage door his *own* agent barred his way.

We soon found out what they meant by going "another way"; it was to use Jack's "sleeping bit," in a cheap imitation, done by another actor.

It took us a long time to get really smart about the blacklist. At first we couldn't figure out who was behind it. It was only when a little newsletter compiling the cases came out that we realized almost every one of the complaints could be traced to a professional red-baiter, Vincent Hartnett (who also made a nice living "clearing"

★★

performers for sponsors and networks), and to a Syracuse supermarket owner named Laurence Johnson. For some reason, Johnson had made it his personal crusade to see that people like Phil Loeb and Jack Gilford were not allowed to work. He would call up sponsors, introduce himself and threaten to take their products off the shelves of his stores if they let "pinkos" like Jack appear on programs they sponsored. Johnson enlisted a Syracuse American Legion post in his crusade; most of the members turned out to be employees of his stores.

We found out only later that Johnson had gone to the Metropolitan Opera while Jack was performing in *Fledermaus* to boast about removing Jack from *The Fred Allen Show* and to demand that Jack be dropped from the cast on the forthcoming Met tour. The Metropolitan was used to dealing with temperamental sopranos and difficult bassos, and a grocer from Syracuse meant nothing to them.

Fledermaus toured in Syracuse, and while she was there visiting Jack, Madeline got hold of Johnson's home phone number.

Madeline knew that Johnson was responsible for having Jack removed from an NBC-TV variety show sponsored by Kellogg's and Pet Milk, but it was hard to prove. When Jack got canceled, she lay down on the couch and thought for three hours—which Jack remembers as the longest time Madeline has been still in the twenty-eight years of their marriage.

Finally, she rose from the couch, went to the phone and called Laurence Johnson at home. She said she was the secretary of Sylvester "Pat" Weaver, the president of NBC, and that she'd found an "urgent" message that Mr. Weaver was to call Mr. Johnson. Could she be of any help with this "urgent" matter? she inquired. Was there anything she could tell Mr. Weaver?

Johnson said he'd never called Sylvester Weaver.

Here's where Madeline's three hours on the couch paid off.

"Oh," she said innocently, "I see something written here in the margin. It says Pet Milk and Kellogg's in Battle Creek. Would this message have anything to do with that?"

"Oh, yes," said Johnson, taking the hook firmly in his mouth. "I called the president of Kellogg's in Battle Creek and the head of Pet Milk in St. Louis. They probably called you. I told them they better not let people like Jack Gilford appear on their show."

"Well," said Madeline, "is there anything we should do?"

"No," said Johnson "it's all taken care of. I've already discussed the whole thing with a program executive."

"Thank you," said Madeline, and hung up the phone.

The next day Jack walked into the office of that executive. He repeated the conversation, and since they could hardly deny it, Jack was offered a return engagement on any of the shows the network controlled, particularly on the late-night *Jerry Lester Show*. When Jack examined the offer carefully, it turned out that he would appear only locally, not on the network segment. But it was work, so he took it.

Madeline and Jack went before the AFTRA committee to press charges. The committee had been formed to hear blacklist evidence. When they arrived, Phil Loeb, who was the committee chairman, jumped up from his chair. There were tears in his eyes. He ran to Jack, grabbed him by his lapels and said, "Jack, don't let them do to you what they did to me."

On another occasion, at an Equity meeting, Phil was asked if it was true that he was a member of Artists Front to Win the War. He answered, "What then, to lose the war?"

In the end their charges all came to nothing. Henry Jaffe, the lawyer for the union, and George Heller, the executive secretary, said nothing could be done since another contract had been offered to Jack to make amends for the blacklisting. Besides, people were saying, you've got other work like *Fledermaus*, so why make trouble?

"Don't make waves" was the prevailing attitude. It was bad enough that you couldn't find work, but in the climate of the times people would cross the street to avoid meeting you. That hurt even worse.

Madeline was once walking down East Fifty-sixth Street with the composer Harold Arlen. Harold and Yip Harburg were writing *Jamaica* in Harold's apartment, and Madeline was assisting with the casting. At a distance Harold looks a little like Jack. Ahead of them they noticed an orchestra conductor they both knew. As he approached Madeline and Harold, he stopped dead in his tracks and made a beeline across the street. Arlen raised his hand in a friendly greeting, and the conductor, recognizing him at last, blanched.

Zero used to say that the only good thing about the blacklist was that since he couldn't work in movies or in television, where they paid good money, he wasn't giving anything up when he did the classy things he loved like Molière at the Brattle Theatre.

And even I got to do some acting during that time. The Brattle was a theater in Cambridge, near Harvard Square. It was founded by a group of Cambridge people and was open fifty-two weeks a year, so they must have been rich. In fact, once, when an actress did something that displeased Zero in a scene and he started to complain, the director rushed up and said, "Shhh, she's Martin's Hot Dogs."

The Brattle did classics and new plays, and occasionally hired outside names like Zero. When they asked him to do *The Imaginary Invalid,* he was happy to accept. Maybe it wasn't in Urdu, but it sure was culture. And when he told them he'd like me to have a part in the play, too, they agreed. They figured they'd have to give something to get a "name" to work for so little money, and since I could walk and talk at the same time they weren't taking much of a chance. The play was a big success for Z and for the theater, and nobody threw anything at me. In addition, I was getting coverage on Blue Cross.

I really love being on the stage. I used to think everyone wanted to be onstage and just some lucky people made it. I was flabbergasted when my friend Emily Paley told me she'd rather die than step out in front of an audience.

Since I was accustomed to being onstage with an orchestra as a kind of buffer between me and the audience, people used to ask me, "Aren't you nervous—you, a dancer—going out onstage and saying words?" Well, I wasn't nervous. I think it was Agnes De Mille who said, "Throw a dancer onstage and tell her where the exit is, and she'll be okay."

A year or so after *The Imaginary Invalid* and *The Doctor in Spite of Himself,* both of which were hits at the Brattle, Albert Marre was sending out what they call "a package"—a touring company that goes out in the summer to various tent theaters as well as theaters in the round in resort areas.

Marre was doing *Three Men on a Horse* and I was to do the Shirley Booth part, which had always been my dream. The stars were Wally Cox and Walter Matthau. Wally, who had become a celebrity for his portrayal of Mr. Peepers, was the first big TV personality to go out on tour with a play. The fans literally besieged him wherever we went. Once, when he was out in a rubber boat in the Atlantic Ocean off Ogonquit, Maine, people swam out to get his autograph, holding their pencils and autograph books above their heads or in their teeth.

The character I played was supposed to have been a Ziegfeld Follies girl, but this was 1953 and there hadn't been a Follies in years. I asked the director if I could make the character a Rockette and he agreed.

One of the critics of the Boston *Herald-American* wrote: "Miss Harkin does a wonderful burlesque of an ex-Rockette going

★★

through a routine. . . ." He didn't know that I *was* an ex-Rockette. (Frank Loesser used to call me the oldest living Rockette.) It was really very funny. Imagine one person all alone on a stage doing what the Rockettes do in the line: left kick, knee left, right kick, knee right, flip kick right, left, right, left, sixteen fan kicks, about-face, kneel front, finish. In a line of thirty-six girls this looks like some miracle of unified motion. When one person does it, it looks like she's headed for the booby hatch.

While I was in *Three Men on a Horse,* the kids were up on Monhegan with my mother and Zero was working in the Catskills, for a change. Once he brought the boys to see me in Ogonquit. They drove down in Herbie Kallem's old car, which had one door that worked and one door that was tied shut and couldn't be opened. Every time one of the kids had to pee, everybody else had to get out. After all that trouble, Zero didn't get to see me in the play because he couldn't get a baby-sitter.

Zero, resourceful soul, almost managed to get by without *ever* coming to see me act (and don't think I ever forgave him). In 1958, come to think of it, he didn't see me in *Damn Yankees,* but when that show closed I filled in for the actress playing Molly Bloom in *Ulysses in Nighttown.* Since he played Bloom, he couldn't help seeing me, I guess.

It wasn't only that Zero didn't take my acting seriously. (Certainly, during the blacklist we needed the $200 I brought in from time to time.) It was that he really wanted me to be home seeing that everything was nice for him, taking care of him and the boys. That was enough of a job for me, he thought.

I wonder if he ever knew that I would have paid those producers to let me act, that's how much I loved to work. But if I hadn't earned a salary Zero wouldn't have baby-sat, so I allowed them to pay me.

At any rate, in the Fifties we had very little choice in these things. Since Zero was blacklisted—from everything but a few classy, underpaid dramas and a club date now and then in the Catskills, where he was often paid half of what he was promised—and since the kids were too young to work, that left me.

At first I thought I wasn't equipped to do anything but dance, and I hadn't danced at all since my first son was born. I took a few lessons when Josh was about three months old, but the combination of seeing myself in the mirror and not being able to jump more than an inch off the floor made me give that up.

I remember exactly when it happened. I was taking ballet class with the most uninspiring, dull teacher I'd ever met, and in the middle of a difficult combination it struck me that I didn't have to do this—besides which I wasn't doing it very well. And even if I were doing it well, it wasn't going to lead anywhere because who's beating the bushes looking for a twenty-eight-year-old slightly overweight ballet dancer?

So I left class quietly—the first quiet thing I'd ever done—and went to the dressing room. I took off my hand-knit heavy wool tights, my dance belt (the female equivalent of a jockstrap, like a girdle with a cloth piece between the legs) and my ballet shoes. I folded the tights and dance belt neatly, got dressed and abandoned them. Somebody, I thought, will be happy to get the hand-knit tights and might even be happy with the ballet shoes, but I was certain no one would grab the dance belt.

That night at the theater I met Nora Kaye (remember *International Casino*?), who had become the foremost ballerina in the country, and I told her what I'd done. Clive Barnes will never believe this, but she said, "Oh God, I wish I could quit."

I'd always wanted to study acting, but I never knew who should have the pleasure of teaching me. Through a friend I found a man named Don Richardson, who was willing to take me as a pupil even though I'd never play Juliet or Lady Macbeth. My goals were modest: I wanted to be the warm-hearted woman who had all the jokes and was a friend of the heroine. Also, if I ever got a passport (and the money to go abroad), where it says Occupation, instead of housewife I wanted to put ACTRESS.

Once I asked Zero to come with me to the lessons, and he sat in for about three of them, I think. But he really didn't need lessons. He could do anything you wanted him to do on the stage. You'd say "Laugh" and he'd laugh, "Cry" and he'd sob. Ask him to do a somersault, anything. He was completely uninhibited as far as acting was concerned. No one ever taught him. He was just an actor. Without any acting lessons.

After you learn to act, you have to get a job acting. That's the hard part. I discovered by watching a friend who did it all the time that the only way to get a part is to ask everyone you meet who's doing a picture or a play or a TV show, "Is there a part in it for me?" If you ask often enough and know enough people, somebody's bound to say yes. And sure enough, one did.

That one was Arthur Laurents, who was in from Hollywood with a play, *The Birdcage*. I asked him the magic question and I finally got a "Sure, come and read for it."

I felt really exposed up there, all alone, with just a worklight and a stage manager to read with me, but since I knew the author, the director, Harold Clurman, and the producer, Wally Fried, it wasn't too terrible, and it was a small part. Anyway, I got it!

Phil Loeb wrote a letter to Zero, who was out of town somewhere, saying, "Kate is in rehearsal, a fact she considers equal in importance to the dropping of the atomic bomb!"

It was true, even though the latest gift to the American theater was only getting a fast $100 a week. Seven years after the Music Hall, I was now one of ten people talking on the stage instead of one of thirty-six kicking in a line.

The Birdcage was a play about four women who worked in

a night club. Elinor Lynn played a magician, Rita Duncan, who was married to Tony Canzonari, was the cigarette girl, and Jean Carson played the girl at the checkroom. Maureen Stapleton was the wife of the owner, who was played by Melvyn Douglas. We were all rather "outspoken," and at lunch one day Douglas confessed that he hadn't heard language such as ours since he'd been in the army. Our hair wasn't too perfect either, apparently. Rita had to dye hers red, and I, of course, was a blonde again, but this time platinum. (Five hours at the hairdresser every two weeks. They paid, but my hair was thankful when we closed.)

Unfortunately, the play folded three weeks after we opened in New York. The only good to come out of it was Maureen Stapleton, whose first big part this was.

And two of my primary life goals were accomplished: the Mostel family was finally on Blue Cross and I got to appear on the stage without dancing.

Birdcage was the only flop Arthur Laurents ever wrote, and I was in it. When you're out of luck, you're really out. The day after it closed I rushed to the hairdresser and was made brunette again. That afternoon Joshua and Tobias came into the living room and Josh said to me, "Are you Kate?"

"No," I said.

He looked again, turned and walked out of the room, muttering, "Funny, you look like Kate."

Of course, I wasn't always lucky enough to get cast in a play. One Christmas during the blacklist, Zero as usual had no real job, so I got work at Saks Fifth Avenue selling toilet seats. They were fancy, hand-painted toilet seats, and they were expensive in Saks' ritzy gift shop. But they were toilet seats nonetheless. I took that job because the kids wanted bicycles for Christmas, and the pay was $50 a week plus about a third off the bikes in Saks' toy department.

Madeline, during the blacklist, worked "under the table"—

on the fringes of show business. She did occasionally get a part in radio and television, but never one that included her appearing by name or face. She usually "appeared" as a voice emanating from a baby or offstage. Recently, in a retrospective TV special about the good old days of TV, I suddenly heard a beagle speaking with the unmistakable voice of Madeline Gilford.

Madeline also handled props, was a stylist and worked as a home economist for commercials. Those were the days when you put baby oil on chocolate icing to make it look better on camera, so she didn't get much to eat. She was also a casting director, and one summer she and Lisa cleaned the rooms in an old store on Tenth Avenue where props were kept for commercials. These odd jobs qualified her for unemployment, and that's what she and Jack (also collecting those checks) lived on for a long time.

When Madeline worked, Jack used to hang out in Zero's studio, bringing baby Joe. Phil, Sam Jaffe and Stanley Prager also called it "home" in the unemployed afternoons. There are some lovely portraits Z painted in those days, including one of Joe at eighteen months.

Once, at the studio, remembering Madeline divorced Mitchell after eight years, Jack jumped up saying, "This is my eighth anniversary. I better run home and see if my option has been picked up."

Under another name, Madeline packaged and produced a popular and very unusual television show called *Sing Along with Charity Bailey*. Charity Bailey was a marvelous black music teacher from the Little Red Schoolhouse, where the Gilford kids were enrolled.

The *New York Times* review of the show said, "Hooray for Channel 4," and the show ran for two years. It was the forerunner of *Sesame Street* and was the first interracial children's show. Madeline got a small royalty to stay away from it. They had enough trouble being interracial; they didn't need someone blacklisted and Jewish hanging around, too.

Jack was in the off-Broadway production of *The World of Sholem Aleichem*, taking home $109 a week. His theory was that they could make it financially if they cut out dentistry and dry cleaning, but at this disastrous point in their financial circumstances Madeline got a job as a waitress in a Village coffeehouse right next to the Circle in the Square theater. Because so many agents and actors frequented the café, Madeline pretended she was only working to learn the coffeehouse business in case she and Jack wanted to "diversify." Like a good actress, she began to believe it herself, and one night, after a customer waited twenty minutes for ketchup and fifteen minutes for a cold hamburger, she was fired.

Madeline was just as glad; the whole thing wasn't working out financially anyhow, since the baby-sitter's mother demanded that her daughter get carfare even though she lived in the same building.

In 1954, our friend Arnaud d'Usseau, who had written *Tomorrow the World* and *Deep Are the Roots* with James Gow, began a play with Dorothy Parker. It was to be called *The Ladies of the Corridor.*

Evidently, the work didn't go smoothly because, as every reader who's gotten this far knows, Dorothy Parker was a drinker. Arnaud wasn't, so to make sure they could work the next day, they had to keep Dorothy away from the bottle the night before. They'd see that she ate (which was important if she wasn't to get loaded) and that she had fun so that she wouldn't feel depressed. That meant after-dinner games.

Dorothy loved parlor games, charades, Botticelli, any game. Every night Sue saw to it that there were people around to play them with her. That's where we came in. Zero didn't really like games, but for Dorothy he made allowances.

★★

I was petrified the first night I was to meet her. If you've read all the devastating things Dorothy Parker said to or about people, you'd have to be a fool not to be scared. I walked in expecting to see an Amazon who would take one look at me, immediately hit upon all my weaknesses and proceed to make mincemeat of them. Instead, I found a Lady.

Dorothy was tiny and had the softest, loveliest voice I ever heard. Her diction was impeccable, and, of course, her choice of words was precise. And the brain behind all of this was formidable. Her head was well filled with the kind of information you needed to play Botticelli, the game of identities in which you think of a famous person, say, Hamlet. But you only give the other players the initial. They have to ask questions such as "Did you write music to be played on water?" and the "H" would say, "No, I'm not Handel." But if that person can't answer, the one who's "It" has to. We all knew musicians, Zero knew obscure painters. But Dorothy knew all kinds of categories. One night she asked an "H," "Do you chase men for business and for pleasure?" and the "H" was stumped and said, "I give up," and Dorothy said, "J. Edgar Hoover." She got a free question, of course.

The game which revealed Dorothy's carefully hidden vulnerable core was Adverbs. In Adverbs the person who is "It" leaves the room and the remaining players select an adverb. The "It" comes back and asks each person to do something in the manner of the chosen word. Walk in the manner of the word, sing a song in the manner of the word, and so on. I remember one night the word was "vulgarly." I crossed the room, and I did bumps and grinds, snake hips, anything else I could think of. When Dorothy was asked to make a speech, she stood up and in a quiet refined voice talked about money. Because the way she was brought up, talking about money was vulgar.

Once she told me that whenever she couldn't sleep she'd try to fit poetry into the song "Inky Dinky Parlez-Vous." Then she added, "Milton always works best." I asked for an example and she sang:

> *"She comes meandering o'er the lee, parlez-vous.*
> *She comes meandering o'er the lee, parlez-vous.*
> *She comes meandering o'er the lee,*
> *The beautiful nymph Euphrosyne.*
> *Inky Dinky Parlez-Vous."*

The regimen of food and fun was so successful that *Ladies of the Corridor* was finished, had a producer and was ready to go into rehearsal in the autumn of 1954.

I was out of town doing summer stock in *Three Men on a Horse* when Arnaud called and asked me to read for a small part as chambermaid in the play. I got it and was glad, though it paid only minimum, then $100 a week. One night in the Russian Tea Room Lenny Lyons asked me what the play was about. I said, "It's a play about a chambermaid." When it was published in book form, the authors gave me a copy and the inscription said, "We still think it's a play about a chambermaid," signed Dorothy Parker and Arnaud d'Usseau.

The night *Ladies* opened we went to a friend's house to wait for the reviews. Zero and I, Arnaud and Sue, Emily Paley and Dorothy. Someone went to Times Square for the papers, and the reviews were not good. Not rotten, but not good. So we were not a jolly group. There's really not much to say when a play you've worked on for over a year gets panned by most of the critics, but we agreed that they all were jerks and didn't know shit from Shinola. As we were getting our coats and saying goodbye, Dorothy said in her lovely soft voice, "Does anybody need a lady pool shark?"

Dorothy went back to Hollywood after that and married Alan Campbell for the second time. (I knew her in between the

Campbells.) Then Alan died and she was alone again. I've been told that when a friend went to the house after the funeral and asked Dorothy if there was something he could do, she replied, "Nothing." He insisted that there must be something he could do, and in desperation she said, "Well, if you insist, go to the corner and get me a tuna on rye, hold the mayo."

Dorothy was unlucky in a lot of ways. For instance, do you know anybody else who bought a string of real pearls for fifty G's as an investment for the future and then was left holding nothing when cultured pearls were invented? She even laughed when she told me. And she had a beautiful Utrillo that she had to sell at a loss during bad times. The year she died she could have gotten a fortune for it.

But Dorothy had class. When we couldn't get a charge account in any department store, or if we had one the store canceled it because of the blacklist, she said, "As soon as you have money, get a charge at Tiffany's and then all the other stores will give you one." And I did. It worked just as she said.

After Alan Campbell died, she came back east and we saw her occasionally. She'd come to the house for dinner and fold the napkins in the shape of animals for the kids as she'd always done, and she'd do her best toward cleaning up by picking up one dish to dry and rubbing it all the time everybody was washing, drying, emptying garbage. She was darling but not domestic.

One day a friend of hers called to tell me Dorothy was in the hospital, having fallen over her dog Misty while getting out of a cab. That must have been Misty VI. She called all her miniature poodles Misty with a number. I went to see her and she seemed in fine spirits, very anxious that Misty not be blamed for her fall. She explained that dogs were always eager to get out of cars when they stopped, and it was her own fault for not being prepared. I had to go to London while she was still in the hospital, and I asked our son

Toby to see that she got home all right when she was discharged. He took the day off from school, commandeered a car with a driver and took her back to the Hotel Volney, where she lived.

She was alone with Misty when she died there about a year later. At the funeral Lillian Hellman spoke, along with Zero. Lillian said that one night in their cups they were trying to decide what should be put on their gravestones, and Dorothy wanted on hers "If you can read this, you're too close."

Arnaud once told me that he and Dorothy and the others had been playing a game on a night when Zero and I weren't there. Everybody was asked to make a guest list for an imaginary dinner party which could include anybody in the world. Dorothy's list contained Pablo Picasso, Sean O'Casey and several other luminaries. When her friends pointed out that those people were all strangers to her and she ought to have at least one person she knew to help keep the conversation flowing, she said, "Then I'll have Kate and Zero, of course." Nothing nicer has ever been said of me.

Because of the blacklist we were all pioneers in a new kind of theater that was emerging all over the country—in tents. One of the most famous and one that consistently employed blacklisted actors was located in Hyannis, Massachusetts, and directed by Bill Ross, who had been the stage manager at *Fledermaus*.

Jack and Phil Loeb appeared in Hyannis in a memorable version of *Charley's Aunt*. Jack played Charley and Phil was the lecherous Mr. Spettigue. Phil put his heart and soul into the part, pursuing Jack, dressed as Charley's aunt, as if he really meant it. They invented some of the funniest business ever seen in that play. At one point, they were seated, coyly, back to back, on a love seat. Mr. Spettigue put his hand on Charley's knee in a hammer-hold, and Jack made a terrible face at the audience—which Phil couldn't see. But with his wonderful sense of timing he followed Jack's grimace with one of his own, then Jack picked up the rhythm and soon they had the audience rolling in the aisles. As they roared, Phil turned to Jack and in a loud stage whisper said, "I'm going to fuck you."

Tent theaters are built to accommodate the fast pace of the action, with ramps for the actors to run up and down on, but in the old theaters the ramps were not gently graded. At Hyannis, Jack had to do a soft-shoe dance in the theater's steep aisles. At the end of the week he was so stiff that Madeline had to lift his legs onto the gas pedal of the car.

Tent theaters never have enough money for complicated sets, and the actors usually make their entrances through the audience, which, when Jack was appearing in *Finian's Rainbow* in Flint, Michigan, caused a problem. A scene in the play calls for the character playing the Senator to suddenly turn black. On Broadway this is handled by letting one of the chorus boys substitute for the Senator, who then gets made up backstage. In a tent they can't spare anyone from the chorus, so the stage would be blacked out and the Senator would race up the aisle, where apprentices would smear him with black make-up as the cast ad-libbed onstage.

On this particular night the Senator went up the wrong aisle at the very moment that a hapless customer started to use the correct aisle to find his way to the bathroom. Under cover of darkness the apprentices grabbed him, and when the lights went up there was a bewildered white Senator in the aisle stage left and the spotlight was on a blacked-up customer wandering around, hands outstretched, calling pitifully, "Harriet . . . Harriet . . ."

In 1949 Garson Kanin wrote a show called *The Live Wire.* Sheila Bond eventually played the lead part of a tough Rockette. (I had auditioned for the part and answered all sorts of questions about the Music Hall, but I guess I wasn't their idea of a Rockette.) Madeline was signed to understudy the lead when the show was out of town, and Kanin had written a special part just for Jack. This was the beginning of a long-lasting relationship between Gar and Jack, which had really started before the war at a Hollywood party where Jack had performed his drunk act. He'd pretended to be drunk to make a really drunk lady feel comfortable. At that party Gar had told Jack, "Someday I'm going to use you in a show."

In *The Live Wire* Jack played a vaudevillian. The show tried out on the road in New England. Ruth Gordon came along to give her advice to her husband, Garson Kanin. Mike Todd, married at that time to Joan Blondell, was the producer of the show. Mike and Joan once showed up at the Riobamba in Chicago when Jack was appearing there. They were the only customers for the last show of the night, and Jack performed for them alone in what must have been an embarrassing half-hour. But they were a good audience, and Jack has always had a secret crush on Joan Blondell.

Live Wire was not a hit in New York. In fact, no one can remember much about the play, but everyone remembers the fun they had on those out-of-town dates. One night, for example, they had a moonlight clambake on the beach at Ogonquit. The entire cast and the Kanins and the Todds were there. Everyone was huddled around the campfire for warmth. At a certain moment, after much beer and many lobsters and clams, a young female scene painter whom no one had really noticed for two weeks took off her glasses, unfurled her long brunette hair, stripped off her blue jeans and shirt and, in a skintight black maillot, ran into the freezing surf. None of the others had ever ventured into that water for fear of turning blue. This young woman not only didn't turn blue, she turned into a sexy mermaid. They were talking about this magical moment long after the play closed.

A little later, Garson called Jack and told him he was involved in a production of *Fledermaus* at the Metropolitan Opera. He didn't want Jack to sing, but to do the opera's only speaking part, that of the drunken jailer, Frosch. Jack said, "Yes, I'd love to do it," but Garson insisted that Jack read the script first. Jack tried to tell him that he knew the part would be fabulous, he wanted to take the job first and then read the script. They argued like this for several minutes until Garson had to explain that Rudolph Bing, director of the Met, wanted to have thirteen different comedians, people like Bobby Clark, Harpo Marx and Milton Berle, play the role in thirteen different performances of the opera.

One of the different comedians was also Zero. Gar had called one day while Z was out and asked me, "Do you think Zero would like to come to us at the Met?" I stuttered that I was sure he would and that Zero would be home at six o'clock that evening. Our conversation closed on a note of great excitement, but, though we waited and waited, Gar never did call back.

As to Jack, he thought Bing's idea of multiple-choice comedians would eliminate him, despite Gar's reassurances that none of the other men was right for the part.

Nineteen-fifty was not a terrific year for Jack, professionally, and when he called Madeline to tell her that he'd just signed for a starring role in *Fledermaus* at the Met, she said, "If you're not too big a star by the time you get home, would you please pick up the clothes at the Laundromat?"

The production was in English, with lyrics by Howard Dietz. Great Metropolitan Opera stars like Richard Tucker, Luba Welitch, Jarmila Novotna, Maria Jeritza, Patrice Munsel and Risé Stevens were among those who eventually sang in the several *Fledermaus* productions which included Jack. It was, I admit, a cut above my experience at the Chicago Opera House.

A few days before the show opened, Jack's mother died. She'd called him backstage once during rehearsal, and he'd held the phone away from his ear to let her listen to the glorious music. Jack was numb with the shock of her death, with the enormity of the role and the elegance of the audience—not to mention the size of the "room" in which he was playing, but which eventually he turned into his own living room as he always did onstage.

Since he didn't appear onstage until the third act, Jack would hang around as long as possible listening to the music. Then, in the middle of the second act, he put on his make-up—a pale face, dark beetle brows, a red nose, of course, with ears to match. He wore the rumpled uniform of a drunken jailer who fell down regularly. His entrance was inspired. He emerged from a jail cell on a balcony above stage level. The cell was full of tarts (the human, not the bakery kind) who clung to Jack as he stepped through the door and fell down a flight of fifteen steps to the stage.

The role of Frosch had been done in Europe by all the important clowns, but after Alfred Lunt saw Jack perform he wrote Gar: "I've seen Grock, the Fratellinis and Slivers and all the best, but none could touch him. How he manages to dissolve, vanish completely, while manacled to the tenor is—I think, the greatest feat of acting I ever saw."

Garson had devised a situation to keep Jack onstage during the entire third act. As the very drunken Frosch, Jack would handcuff himself to the tenor and then, while the tenor sang a spirited trio, would manage to make it seem that he wasn't there. Leaning drunkenly, he would let himself be dragged across the stage between choruses, hanging limply from the tenor's hand, making no movement except to tip his hat.

As the drunken jailer, he also delivered the morning report to the audience. This became a kind of verbal cadenza, the equivalent of the virtuoso parts the singers had in which they could show off their high notes and trills. Jack improvised some of the funniest material of his career on the great stage of the Metropolitan. He would stand alone midstage, find a bottle of booze in the tuba, attempt to conduct the orchestra and generally have a wonderful

137

****
170 YEARS OF SHOW BUSINESS

time—as did the orchestra and the audience.

Playing Frosch gave Jack a chance to do a lot of loud, low comedy that was very different from the kind of material he was used to. He still considers it the most enjoyable and funniest part he's ever done. *Fledermaus* played to audiences throughout the country over a period of fifteen years with Jack in the role of Frosch. It was, for many years, the traditional New Year's Eve show at the Met in New York.

When Jack got the part, he was front-page news all over New York, but this was a mixed blessing because it also made him a target for the newly developing blacklist.

One day Rudolph Bing called him into his office. "My dear Gilford," he said, "it seems that a man from Syracuse has told us you are connected with Communist things and that you have contributed money to *The Daily Worker.*" Jack responded that he hadn't given the *Worker* any money but that he had entertained for various left-wing causes and perhaps notice of these performances had appeared in the *Worker*. Mr. Bing, an Austrian refugee from Hitler, didn't care about anyone's politics, though he was worried that there might be trouble for him and for his company from the people accusing Jack. He stood firm and had one of his associates, Reginald Allen, write a letter to Laurence Johnson in Syracuse to that effect.

Jack wasn't fired. Not then, anyhow. The show went on tour, and even in Syracuse, where Johnson had threatened to picket the Loew's theater at which *Fledermaus* was playing, there was no trouble.

Jack loved performing in *Fledermaus* so much that, until 1967, he included a clause in every contract he signed releasing him so that he could play Frosch.

One night a man came backstage at the Opera asking for Mr. Gellman. It was Milton Berle, of course, come to say that he thought the Met was a "good room" for Jack. He added that he'd never heard so much low laughter from so many high-class people.

Both the Mostel boys, I'd like to say here, have also appeared at the Met. Toby and Josh were at P.S. 166 when the Met asked for children who'd be interested in singing in the children's chorus. The kids tried out and were chosen, and I waited for them after the first rehearsal.

"What opera are you learning?" I asked Toby.

"Boris Karloff," he replied.

The kids got $3 for a performance. Josh used to walk from the old Met on Fortieth Street and Seventh Avenue to Times Square. By the time he got to Eighth Avenue he'd had some pizza, a couple of hot dogs, something liquid to wash them down and a little snack to tide him over for the next block's journey. He ate his way through the $3 every single night, and he gained twenty pounds that season.

In 1952 Madeline and Jack decided it was time to have a baby—blacklist or no blacklist. Joe Gilford was born on December 6. He had rather dark skin, black hair which stood straight up around his head and the wizened face of an old man. He was not a beautiful baby, but by some miracle of time, vitamins and latent genes he's turned out to be a handsome grown man.

Aside from *Fledermaus* and a few bit parts out of town, Jack had had no work for months. The Gilfords owed the hospital $250, and although Madeline could have gone home anytime, the hospital wouldn't let Joe go. They were holding him for ransom against the unpaid bill.

Jack—ever the proud Rumanian—would not borrow money even from his closest friends, and for a while it looked like Joe Gilford would spend the rest of his life in the nursery. Just then, a friend of Jack's offered him a day's work in a movie called *From*

Main Street to Broadway. It was being made in New York and featured a lot of big stars in small roles, people like Ethel and Lionel Barrymore, Tallulah Bankhead and Gertrude Berg. Jack played the part of a nervous box-office man, the shooting took one day, Jack got $500 and Joe Gilford was sprung.

They hadn't planned on a boy and so had no name picked out. The *Variety* announcement simply said a baby boy had been born to Jack and Madeline Gilford.

On the same page there was a memorial notice to mark the first anniversary of the death of J. Edward Bromberg, a blacklisted actor friend of the Gilfords'. Bromberg had a bad heart, and, though the doctors warned against it, he testified as an "unfriendly" witness at Committee hearings. Then, broken physically and spiritually, he went to England to try to get work. He was in a Dalton Trumbo play in London, and his wife and three children were on their way to join him, when, at the age of forty-eight, he had a massive heart attack and died. Joe Gilford, who was born on December 6, 1952, was named for Joe Bromberg, who died on December 6, 1951.

The insidious thing about the blacklist was that although we *could* sometimes work on Broadway—and more often off-Broadway —movies and television were closed to us and without that exposure it was hard to get the few well-paying jobs in the New York theater. It was ironic that people were permitted to pay to see Zero or Jack in a play but were not supposed to see them on free TV. They were supposed to turn their sets off whenever by some fluke one of those "subversives" did manage to get a minor role and were even supposed to boycott the products made by sponsors of such shows.

In the fall of 1955, right after the HUAC hearings in New York and with the shock of Phil's suicide fresh and sharp in our minds, Jack went into rehearsal for *The Diary of Anne Frank.* The play gave Jack his first chance at a serious role, that of the elderly, fussy, frightened dentist, Mr. Dussel, who closeted with the Frank family in their Amsterdam attic. Keeping the character true-to-life yet sympathetic was a challenge for Jack, but he was devoted to the role and to the play. *Anne Frank* won every prize possible, and Jack stayed in it for two years—as long as the real Dussel had stayed in the attic. The Boris Aronsen set was so detailed a replica of the actual Frank residence that, years later, when the Gilfords visited it in Amsterdam, Jack felt as if he'd really lived there.

Jack's next Broadway part, one of the two soldiers in Peter Ustinov's *Romanoff and Juliet,* was not as good a role, but it was a chance to work with Ustinov and with George S. Kaufman, the director. When people asked Jack why he took such a minor part after *Anne Frank,* Jack responded rationally, "I have three children." (It's worth adding here that Jack once came up to Zero and told him with great excitement that little Joe had begun to talk. His first words: "Mama," "Papa" . . . "blacklist.")

Romanoff and Juliet had many written laugh lines, but Jack and Phil Leeds were two old stand-up comics who couldn't resist adding things to their meager roles. At one point in the play they sang a sea song to Juliet's balcony, and to add a little humor they would rock while they sang, as if they were in a boat. When the show first opened, Ustinov sat quietly on a bench at the side of the stage, aloof, observing them. Pretty soon, however, their little boat shtick seemed to be getting more and more laughs at the wrong places. Puzzled, Jack asked Madeline to come to the performance and tell him why the audience was laughing. Madeline discovered that Ustinov, out of sight of Jack and Phil, was rowing the bench he sat on like a canoe with a long pantomime paddle.

Jack also played in *Look After Lulu,* an adaptation of a Feydeau farce which was Noel Coward's last play for Broadway. It did not get good notices, but it won stardom for Tammy Grimes and Jack had the joy of working with Noel Coward—not only a brilliantly

141

****

170 YEARS OF SHOW BUSINESS

talented man but one of the warmest, most tender, most considerate human beings Jack had ever met. Jack had admired Coward since he was very young and had kept the program from *Bittersweet,* which he'd been taken to see when he was a boy. When Jack asked him to autograph the program, Coward got tears in his eyes and said, "They liked my plays more then."

There's a show business saying to console actors who have only a few lines: "There are no small parts, only small actors." To which we always add: "And small salaries." But Jack had two of his greatest successes in plays in which he spoke only one line: he was the painfully shy Bonche Schweig in *The World of Sholem Aleichem* and he played the mute king Sextimus in *Once upon a Mattress,* in which Carol Burnett made her debut. In 1964 and 1972 *Mattress* was a TV special, and Jack was one of the two members of the original cast to be included.

After *Mattress,* Jack was a last-minute replacement during rehearsals of Paddy Chayefsky's *The Tenth Man.* He had only read one line—two different ways—when director Tyrone Guthrie said, "Mr. Gilford, you are with us." He played the part for two years on Broadway.

Jack is a man who thinks he needs lots of cuing when he's learning a part. Traditionally, the person chosen as cuer is—without audition—the actor's wife. Cuing is a very boring job—take it from those who've done it. And since it's usually done at night, cuers (and sometimes cuees) have been known to fall asleep. These teams are so often married to each other that the cuing process can sometimes take place in the most comfortable part of the house, bed. In fact, many actors can't learn their parts standing up.

When Jack was offered a part in *No, No, Nanette,* he was appearing in *The Price* in Buffalo. Consequently, he didn't have much time to learn the role, and that made him nervous. During a *Nanette* rehearsal break in Baltimore, Madeline was cuing him while

Jack was lying on a leather couch in the lobby. He must have looked pathetic because Madeline said: "I think you're having a nervous breakdown and should go to a hospital. Then you can legally get out of this contract."

That did it. Jack pulled himself together. He's never missed a performance, except for a bout of bleeding ulcers during the run of *Forum*, and although he opened in a stupor he continued to do the role in *Nanette* for a year. On his closing night, December 31, 1971, the cast gave him a Purple Heart: a golden medallion with an amethyst heart in the center, suspended from a purple ribbon and engraved from Ruby Keeler, Patsy Kelly, Bobby Van and Helen Gallagher for "Bravery Beyond the Call of Duty," a tribute to his forbearance in a difficult role.

Jack was in Neil Simon's *The Sunshine Boys* when his nomination came through for an Academy Award for Best Supporting Role in *Save the Tiger* with Jack Lemmon. He got two nights off to go to the ceremony, and he bought a new pair of black patent-leather shoes. He didn't win the award, and after it was all over, Madeline, noticing the unscratched shoe soles, said, "I wonder if you can return them."

Jack was also in the film *Harry and Walter Go to New York*. He played a lot of nice scenes with Diane Keaton, most of which were left on the cutting room floor. He had better luck earlier in his roles in *Enter Laughing, The Incident* and *Catch-22*, in which he played Dr. Daneeka.

In 1963 he finally began to get a few parts in television. His first post-blacklist show was a special for children, *The Cowboy and the Tiger*. Then, slowly, the shows began to seep back, first at the exasperating rate of one or two a year. But then he was cast as an old man who illegally made wine for his cronies in a Jewish home for the aged on the two-hour season opener of the TV series *The Defenders*. After that, Jack began to do more and more TV. Soon he was a regular on the Dean Martin and Carol Burnett shows, and one Monday night in 1976 there was an unofficial Jack Gilford festival on television when he starred in three top national network shows, *Dinah Shore, Rhoda* and *All in the Family.*

In 1962, while Jack was in the Broadway production of *Forum,* his agent got him an audition for a commercial. The audition was held in an ad agency office, it was filmed with a hand-held camera and, all in all, the conditions were not very good. The product? Crackerjacks. Jack says now that the Crackerjack audition may have been the most important of his career.

He was the Crackerjack spokesman for eleven years, and although it's been six years since the last one was shown, Jack still cannot walk down the street in any city in this country, or ride on a train, bus or plane, without someone recognizing him because of that commercial. To this day, people of all ages come up to him and say, "Hey, aren't you the guy used to do that Crackerjack commercial?"

The material was marvelous, and the ads were produced and shot as if they were feature films by an Oscar-winning cameraman for *The Miracle Worker.* They won prizes all over the world.

You may remember the one where Jack is sitting at a table playing poker with a group of card sharks. Jack is a mild-mannered obvious "mark" and the other fellows are beating the pants off him. But Jack just keeps smiling amiably while losing. Then a little box of Crackerjacks is passed around, and when it gets to Jack he tips it into his hand—only to find the box empty. Deprived of Crackerjacks, the mild-mannered country bumpkin turns into a raving lunatic. He lifts up the table and overturns it. The last scene shows a litter of cards and chips and players on the floor as a voice says, "Next time, get the Party-Pak."

In 1955 Jack and Zero did *Once Over Lightly,* their first show together. It was directed by Stanley Prager and co-starred blacklisted Sono Osata as well as our own two favorite "subversives." Yip Harburg suggested calling it *The Banned Wagon.* Another suggested title was *Blacklist Follies.* Mel Brooks wrote some of the sketches, but Jack and Zero wrote a lot of their own material, too. In one hilarious skit Zero, dressed in a Lord Fauntleroy suit, did a musical number called "The Visit of the Kreplach." It was a Yiddish Gian Carlo Menotti opera, written by Marshall Barer, and those who saw it still think it's one of the funniest things Zero ever did.

7

★★★

Zero had very high standards about acting, and there were only a handful of actors he really admired. His idols were Chaplin, Buster Keaton, W. C. Fields and the French actor Raimu. There were several Americans—Marlon Brando and Laurette Taylor, for instance—whom he greatly admired. He would go to watch Jack, whom he loved, but he almost never went to the theater or the movies. There wasn't much he really wanted to see. One winter, though, he took me to three plays in one week. I thought I had a brain tumor and he was only making my last week pleasant.

Zero didn't even have a great feeling for English actors, the way most theater people do. He used to say, "Yes, they can do everything. Only they can't make you cry." He admired actors like Laurence Olivier and Ralph Richardson, but they didn't rank with Chaplin or Keaton in his eyes.

I wasn't with Zero when he met Chaplin at a party at Sam Spiegel's house. Where was I? Taking care of the kids. That's where I always was when anything interesting happened. Zero and Chaplin became great friends right away. They just told each other jokes, and everything went along swimmingly. They didn't get to see much of each other, of course, because Chaplin moved to Europe. But once we had the suite next to Chaplin's at the Savoy, and we went to the opening night party of *A Countess from Hong Kong*, which he made with Sophia Loren and Marlon Brando.

A few years ago the Film Society of Lincoln Center gave Chaplin a party for his eighty-third birthday, and Zero and I went with the Gilfords in a rented limousine which had a faulty jump seat. When Madeline sat down on it, the seat hit me in the leg and gave me a bruise and a golf ball–sized lump so that I had to sit out most of the festivities. There was a cocktail reception after the performance and I was stuck at the table with my bad leg on a chair, but I guess Zero and Charlie had a laugh or two together. There's a picture of them in which they seem to be enjoying each other.

In a pause during the ceremonies, Jack stood up in his seat and yelled, "Welcome back, Charlie!" The next day Jack was at "21," the New York restaurant, and there was Chaplin. Jack is usually a shy fellow, but when it came to Chaplin, who was his idol, too, he couldn't help himself.

He went up to Chaplin's table and said, "Mr. Chaplin, my name is Jack Gilford and I'm an actor and I just wanted to thank you for all you've given us. I, too, was blacklisted and now we're both alive and well in New York and we've all lived for the day when you'd come back."

Chaplin thanked him nicely and said, "You know, a lady wrote me a letter saying that when I got to be eighty I should keep warm. So I'm keeping warm."

As a reply it was a non sequitur but it was very sweet.

Zero and I went to France in 1966 to try to get the rights to Pagnol's *The Baker's Wife*, in which Raimu had played, because Zero thought it would make a good musical, but a lot of other people did, too, and Zero never did get the rights. Pagnol and Zero talked about how great Raimu was, and Pagnol said that Raimu had no idea why he was a great actor or how he did anything. He'd had no training. He'd never studied. He'd just acted. Then, when he read the critics and they said he was great, he knew he'd done it right.

In a *New York Times* piece written after Z died, Jack remembered during the stage version of *Forum* "when a Roman soldier announced the arrival of the 'great General Miles Gloriouses,' Zero fixed a demonic eye on the messenger and sent the actor playing the soldier into a laughing fit. As he exited backstage the soldier shed his uniform and donned a monk's robe and re-entered in a flash from the opposite side. Zero closed in for the kill. Hood hiding his face, the soldier-turned-monk bowed to avoid Zero's eye. The lower the monk bent, the lower Zero bent, until Zero's head was on the floor. Looking up into the hooded face, Z said, "Don't you have a brother in the army?"

Jack was always in awe of writers and didn't realize that he was, in fact, a writer himself. When he came back from the war and thought he didn't have any new material, he simply shut himself into his room for a couple of weeks and came out with several newly created—i.e., written—characters.

Living rooms, beaches, restaurant tables—all became incubators for Jack's material. One of the most felicitous environments for Jack's creativity was the Harburgs' living room. Here he created his White Russian reactionary "Mr. Dmitri" and refined the part every time he visited the Harburgs. Edelaine simply had to say, "Is Mr. Dmitri here?" and Jack would turn into the character and think up new funny stuff for him to say.

Jack does a routine in which he gets increasingly seasick while singing a song of the sea. He'd first learned how to turn green while reading a St. Patrick's Day recipe for green whipped cream.

That was too seasonal a bit for him, so a sea chanty was written for him.

At Camp Copake, a resort where Jack worked as a young man, one of the guests encouraged him to expand some strange conversation they would have. Every night, walking home through the woods, at a certain place Jack would see a space above the trees. There he would halt and begin to talk to God. He'd hold long, funny, companionable talks with God every night and used this bit for years in night clubs and onstage.

As a mimic Jack felt himself actually turning into the characters he played. They got so deeply into him that once in a while, catching a glimpse of himself in a mirror, he'd be surprised to see Jack Gilford instead of Oliver Hardy or Jimmy Durante looking back. Sometimes, elaborating on straight imitations, he would do variations. Imagine, if you will, John D. Rockefeller, Sr., imitating Durante through his thin lips while giving out dimes to the public.

One day in Montreal Jack found himself on the same bill with one of his mimicry "victims," Rudy Vallee. Vallee insisted that Jack do the imitation, and Jack introduced the bit by saying, "Now, with the permission of the copyright owner, I'd like to do Rudy Vallee."

Years later he was imitating Charles Laughton doing the boogie-woogie when at a corner table he noticed Laughton himself, two fists holding up his double chins. Laughton was shaking his head from side to side and mouthing, soundlessly but very clearly, "Shame on you."

Jack is not much for going on at length about how he worked, and not much has been written about Zero's "theories" on acting, either. Maybe that's because Zero got bored quickly giving interviews and he really hated *talking* about acting. He also gave lousy interviews because he never listened to the questions. After seeing

him on TV once, where he was answering the questions he thought
should have been asked and not paying any attention to the inter-
viewer, the kids begged him never to do that kind of show again.
They were embarrassed.

Zero was supposed to do *Rhinoceros* in London. Oscar
Loewenstein, an English producer, had shown it to Zero when he
met him in London, and Z had loved it. But then in February 1959
Z got out of a taxi in front of our house and was hit by a bus, which
caught his leg between the curb and the front wheel. He was in the
hospital for four months, had five operations and for the rest of his
life his leg gave him trouble. After every show (and particularly a
strenuous performance such as he gave in *Fiddler*), Zero's dresser,
Howard Rodney, would massage his bad leg with special creams and
lotions. No one was allowed in the dressing room until Howard had
gently removed Zero's shoe and sock and examined his leg. The
operations had left it with almost no feeling, so Zero couldn't tell
if he'd injured himself onstage. And the circulation was so bad that
the leg would be hot until Howard massaged it back to its normal
temperature. This was a nightly ritual. If he strained too much, as
he did while carrying Peter O'Toole down a flight of stairs in the
film *The Great Catherine*, the graft on his leg split open and he had
to stay in bed for six weeks while it healed.

When he came home from the hospital after that accident, he had to stay in bed a good part of every day. Now, Zero
alone could solve the unemployment problem in New York, just
keeping people waiting on him. Thus, when he said to me one
morning, "Why don't you laugh any more? When I first met
you you were always laughing," I said, "Married to you, it could
happen to a hyena."

Rhinoceros was done in London without him (Laurence
Olivier played his part), but in November the producer, Leo Kerz,

got the rights for *Rhinoceros* in America and asked Zero to play another, smaller part. It was only two scenes, and Eli Wallach was to play the part Zero had originally been asked to do.

Zero played the character who turned into a rhinoceros on-stage. The part is written so the actor can leave the set, go offstage, put a little green make-up on and reenter the scene. This business took place a number of times, and by the end of the scene the character was to have a full rhinoceros make-up on.

Zero didn't want to do it with make-up. He never used make-up; one eyebrow pencil lasted him his entire career. He claimed he could make it as effective without using anything. The director, Joe Anthony, agreed, and so did Leo Kerz. And so did Richard Watts in his *New York Post* review: "The most extraordinary performance of the evening is contributed by Zero Mostel as an exuberant fellow who hastens to conform. Mr. Mostel is probably the only actor in the world who can believably transform himself into a rhinoceros before your eyes without the use of make-up. The lack of any need to rush off stage or hide behind a desk to put on greasepaint in the manner of a stock company thespian changing from Dr. Jekyll to Mr. Hyde adds vastly to the play's effectiveness. Furthermore, Mr. Mostel is highly amusing."

Instead of opening out of town, the play did previews in New York. Another innovation was Leo Kerz's unorthodox decision not to use the critics' comments (if they turned out to be favorable) in an ad. He wanted to woo the theater-going public away from their dependency on critics. He didn't approve of the power critics had (and, we should add, still have today) over what does and does not make it on Broadway. Anyhow, nobody involved with *Rhinoceros* thought the critics would pay much attention since it was, for the time, a new kind of play.

Well, they were wrong. The critics raved, and Leo was stuck

with his principled stand. So he had all the reviews made up into a booklet which you got with your ticket. Or, if you were a prospective ticket buyer, you could pick it up at the box office of the Longacre Theater. It was a lot better than an ad using quotes, since it printed every rave review in full. At the end of the booklet Leo Kerz explained his principles and then thanked all the people who "formed a line at the box office two weeks before the reviews were written."

In fact, getting people to the box office was not without its problems. On Forty-fourth and Forty-fifth streets you get "walkers," that is, people who can't get into any other show on the street (where there are many theaters) and come to you by default. On Forty-eighth Street there's only the Longacre, so anyone walking there is either heading for your show or not looking for the kind of show that's in a theater.

Nevertheless, *Rhinoceros* ran six months, then toured, and Z got such glowing notices that it really made him a big theater star and earned him his first Tony award.

People always ask the wife of a comic (if they notice her at all, which they only do if she's trailing immediately behind her husband like a good squaw): "Is he funny at home?" I think the only answer possible is the Henny Youngman response to "How's your wife?" which is "Compared to what?"

I'll give you a few outstanding examples of the sort of thing you might have in mind and then you can judge:

(1) The first fight I had with Zero after we married, I got very angry and told him to leave. He said, "Okay," then went into the bedroom and made loud packing noises, after which he came out carrying a window pole, completely nude except for his socks and a bow tie that was *not* tied around his neck. Funny?

(2) Zero fancied himself a great cook. He read cookbooks

before he went to sleep, subscribed to *Gourmet* magazine and considered himself a great authority on cuisine.

One Sunday, when the kids were about twelve and fourteen
years old, inspired by the *New York Times* cooking page he announced that he would make dinner. I said, "Fine," only too glad
to get out of any cooking, and he took his *Times* and went into the
kitchen. Three hours later he called us to dinner and served us, in
soup plates, large helpings of something he called *garbure.*

He was the kind of nudgy cook who asks, "How is it?"
before you've even sat down. "How is it, Josh? How is it, Toby?
It's called *garbure.*" They tasted it, and Toby said, "Ugh." Josh
said, "It should be called gar*bage,*" and Zero picked up a knife
and chased Josh around the table. He took away the plates and
said, "All right, if you won't eat it, I will. It's delicious." So he
did. Sunday, Monday, Tuesday, until he finished the swill. He
didn't speak to any of us during all this time, but he never tried
to make it again. Three days of *garbure* was too much even for
him. Is that funny?

(3) Zero was a mad purchaser. A sale anywhere was like a Call
of the Wild to him. He'd be there bright and early, and a good
salesman could sell him anything.

I was sitting at home with a friend one afternoon when Zero
came storming in.

"Wait till you see what I've got!" he yelled the moment he
opened the front door. Then he appeared in the doorway and asked,
"D'you notice anything?"

We both looked, wondering what jewel he had managed to
find that day.

"Is it in plain view?" I asked.

"Yes," he said, and we continued inspecting him till we got
to his feet. My friend got there first and started to giggle, and when
I got there I was dumfounded. On his little feet were the brown

patent-leather and tan kid shoes of an Eighth Avenue pimp. How they were rerouted to Saks Fifth Avenue I can't explain, but there they were, on Zero's feet, and he was happy as a clam.

"Look how light they are," he said as he did a little jog around the room. "They weigh nothing. These were the only pair they had. I got there just in time."

I said, "Z, you went to Saks to get underwear. How did you get to the shoe department?"

"It's right next-door," he said, "and the salesman told me they just came in but they only had one pair so they were put in the sale, too. Aren't they great?"

I wasn't going to tell him they'd look better on a shifty-eyed race track tout, so I agreed with him. "Swell," I said.

He danced happily into his room and kept them on throughout dinner. I don't know when during the evening they started to hurt him, but I never saw him wear those shoes again. Funny?

(4) When we went on a month-long vacation to Europe during *Fiddler*, we had a carefully planned itinerary, including *sixty-six* museums. We had also carefully studied *Shopping in Europe*, which advised us that in Ireland gentlemen who wanted the finest could have shoes made to order. In Dublin, after we unpacked my two lace blouses from Belgium, a petit-point evening bag from Austria, an antique clock from Switzerland and two suits from Paris (that turned out to be too warm for any climate), we raced to the recommended shoestore.

The bootmaker was a delightful and witty conversationalist, and after drawing an outline of Zero's foot on brown paper and taking careful measurements he said he would ship the shoes to New York within three months. We shook hands all around, each outdoing the other in charm, and left the store.

A block down the street Zero stopped. "I only ordered brown," he said. "Maybe I should get a black pair, too."

"Go ahead," I said, feeling a little guilty about all the prizes I'd picked up. "We'll go back."

So we did. Z ordered the black shoes, and after another sprinkling of Irish jollity we went back to the hotel.

The shoes arrived within three months. Zero told all of us that they were here, then put on the brown pair and left for the day. He had alerted everyone he knew to send tracings of their feet on brown paper to Dublin's finest bootmaker.

The night he wore the shoes he came home with a worried look on his face. Everything about him telegraphed catastrophe.

"Listen, Kate," he said, "I don't want to worry you, but something's wrong with my leg. It's throbbing and I'm afraid it'll split open. I've got to call Dr. Wilder."

Joe Wilder told him to come to his house right away. He was worried, too. The symptoms sounded very strange.

"Okay," I said, ever the helpmate. "But do me a favor. Change your shoes, they may be too tight."

"Jesus," he said, "you never believe me when I say I'm sick. You always think I'm a hypochondriac. I tell you, even Joe is worried."

What does a wife do in such a situation? She backs down. And that's what I did. Zero returned to say that Joe had found nothing wrong with him but Z should keep him informed.

The next day he took a martyred bath, ate a martyred breakfast and left his martyr's home.

When he came home that night, he bounced in as he usually did, all bubbling and excited about something else he could buy if he was there early the next morning, and when I asked how his leg was he said, "Oh, fine." He went down the hall to go into his room, and I called after him. "Zero, it was those shoes, wasn't it?" He didn't answer. The next time I saw them, he was asking Josh to try them on.

Another sometimes funny thing is, we learned that the price

of fame is losing a lot of your privacy. Strangers don't think twice about coming up to you in the street and starting a conversation. People had a particularly strange attitude toward Zero. They acted as if they owned a little piece of him. One day, for instance, a bus stopped and a lady got off. Waiting at the stop was Zero. She patted him on the shoulder and said, "Take care of yourself, Zero, take care of yourself." And once Z was walking down the street, as usual not wearing a coat even though it was a nasty, wet day, when an elderly lady walked right up to him and said, "Young man, you should have a coat on." Zero said, "Mind your own business." "Fresh, too," the lady replied, and walked off. He was always bumping into nice old ladies like that.

Come to think of it, I have good street stories, too. Once there was a terrible drunk coming at me on Amsterdam Avenue. I had my hands loaded with packages, was struggling to get home, and as this drunk walked by he said, "Those are *the* most sensible shoes I ever saw." I'll have him know they were my best British walkers. My British Cripplers, I called them.

Those of us who live with comedians sometimes get sucked into playing straight man—without our prior consent. Over the years we've gotten used to it and even quite good at it. Madeline is adept at feeding Jack the lines which turn him into the slippery man who changes his mind, a character he developed at Camp Copake and perfects in the Gilford kitchen while they're fixing supper together.

But once, when they were first married, Jack caught Madeline up in a routine without warning. They were in a liquor store buying a bottle of wine for a romantic candlelight supper.

"What kind of wine is that?" Jack asked the store owner.

"It's Californian," the man replied.

"It's Californian!" Jack screamed into Madeline's ear. "It's a wine from California!"

"A Californian wine!" the liquor man shouted at Madeline,

mouthing the words with a pitying expression on his face.

The man looked so stricken at the thought that this pretty little blonde was deaf, Madeline didn't have the heart to disillusion him. And so the two men continued to shout the entire wine-buying transaction while Madeline stood demurely by. She could hardly have said at that point, "Listen, I'm not deaf. I'm just married to this lunatic comedian."

When they got outside, in a feeble attempt to get back at him Madeline said, "That man is probably thinking, That little girl can't do any better than a moth-eaten fellow like that because she's deaf. Poor thing."

One evening during the run of *Forum*, a friend rented a private room in Sardi's East for a little birthday dinner for his wife, after which we would watch the Academy Awards on a huge TV screen.

The dinner went smoothly, the drinks flowed, the presents were opened and at last the Oscars started. You know how they photograph everyone coming into the auditorium?

Suddenly on the screen appeared John Wayne, making his entrance all smiles, all teeth and all reactionary. Our friends naturally began to boo—what else do you do when John Wayne appears—and from the back of the room ran a slightly tipsy Madeline right to the TV, whereupon she threw her drink in John Wayne's face. We cheered and yelled and laughed, not noticing Jack, who ran like a deer to the TV, wiped the screen off with his handkerchief and said to John Wayne, still on camera, "Madeline didn't mean it."

That was the same night Elizabeth Taylor's new diamond, about the size of a lemon, made its TV debut. The ladies had their noses on the TV screen, inspecting it as minutely as they could, when Zero stood up, banged his spoon on a glass to get attention and bellowed, "I wanted to buy that diamond for Kate, but that son of a bitch Burton outbid me by fifty dollars."

157

****

170 YEARS OF SHOW BUSINESS

And it isn't enough that you have to be onstage with them. They work through the kids, too. Jack used to teach Joe how to do an acting exercise called sense memory, a form of pantomime used in method acting. Jack and Joe, for instance, would hold tea parties with imaginary cups and saucers and tiny imaginary spoons. Joe got quite adept at this game.

One day, while Madeline was fussing with Baby Sam, Joe went to work in the kitchen and made a terrible mess on the floor, spilling assorted boxes of food and cleaning supplies all over the place. Madeline sent Joe for the broom to clean up what he'd done. He came back into the kitchen with his hands precisely fitted around an invisible broom.

He "handed" the broom to Madeline, who yelled, "No, Joe, where's the real broom?"

To which the comedian's child replied, "You must have dropped it, Mommy."

The spouses of actors get involved with their wives' or husbands' careers in other, more important ways, of course. Since actors' lives are run from the phone at home and many decisions about whether or not to accept a job are made over the dinner table after a day of reading a new script, we can't help but be a real part of their working world. Careers have been made, or broken, by helpmates saying "Take it" or "Are you crazy?"

Then, when the show goes into rehearsal, we really get into the act. Our domestic lives have to fit into rehearsal, performing and touring schedules. The Gilford kids were flabbergasted to learn that not everyone ate Thanksgiving dinner at Sardi's so that Daddy could work the holiday matinée show. And by some inborn fluke, actors' kids always manage to get born on opening nights or to have accidents on matinée days when Daddy is away.

Yes, but you lead such glamorous lives, you say. Well, whenever Z was in some exotic or exciting place, where was I? Home with somebody's chicken pox or packing the place to move or attending the kids' Christmas play.

When kids get into trouble, the guys are usually out of town and major decisions are made via long distance. If you can reach them. Often you have to make the decision yourself as if you were a parent-without-a-partner because your partner is off in a different time zone.

Anne Jackson once told Madeline, after being unable to reach her husband, Eli Wallach, in India: "You know, of the sixteen years Eli and I have been married, he's been gone for nine."

In that marriage both partners travel. Madeline once encountered Eli in Bloomingdale's looking completely lost. The poor man had been assigned to buy his teenage daughter her first bra while Anne was out on tour. He coped.

Madeline, despite it all, is an ardent feminist, perhaps because she learned firsthand about the reality of whose role is whose. Long before the liberated seventies, we acting people did what we had to in order to keep the domestic act together. As we've seen, Jack diapered while Madeline politicked.

When Zero and Jack (we called them "the Odd Couple") were together in Spain shooting *Forum*, they were inseparable. Every morning the same car would pick them up at their hotels for the ride out to location. The two of them had lunch together in Zero's trailer. The rest of the company ate like they do at summer camp, standing in a chow line, but Zero lived like a regular movie star, with a trailer and chauffeur. And he insisted Jack be with him constantly.

At night they'd go to their rooms to dress, then meet again and go out to dinner—which in Spain is served around ten. Now, when you're making a movie, the day starts as early as possible to take advantage of the light. These two facts are incompatible, but

Zero and Jack managed to find a few restaurants whose managers, out of the goodness of their hearts, let them in for dinner at eight-thirty so the actors could be in bed by eleven.

They usually had a marvelous time together, but there was one thing Zero did that drove Jack crazy. It drove me crazy for about thirty-five years. Zero had no sweet tooth. He liked fancy pickles, exotic mustard and vinegars made from rare aged sherries. Candy, soft drinks, ice cream—none of these had ever attacked the enamel of his pearly whites. Jack, on the other hand, is like me, a lover of sweets. Every night they'd have a sane dinner of fish or chicken with regulation salad and vegetables, after which Zero would say, "Jack, aren't you going to have dessert?" Jack would try to decline, but finally he'd order the richest, most caloric, most sinfully delicious dessert the restaurant offered. Meringues, flaming soufflés, mousses both chocolate and orange, pastries, flan—whatever was sweet, gooey and guaranteed fattening. Jack secretly looked forward to that moment the way a kid waits for Santa Claus.

In what became an almost sinister game, every single night, without exception and without mercy, when whatever it was came to the table, Zero would say, "Let me have a taste." He'd take a spoonful, then say, "Ugh," or "Yuk, how can you eat that stuff?" or something equally charming. Jack would flip his cork. "Why does he have to taste it every night?" he'd say. "He knows he's going to hate it, so why does he taste it every night?"

One other little idiosyncrasy of Zero's became clear to Jack on that movie set. Whenever we went to a hotel, no matter how grand our room or suite, Zero would always imagine that every other room was better. Whenever a door opened, he'd look in and say, "Look at that suite. It's much nicer than ours." In Spain he had a fancier room than anyone working on that film. Jack had nice but much more modest accommodations in a smaller hotel down the

160

****

MOSTEL/GILFORD

street. And guess where Zero napped in the afternoons when it rained? On Jack's bed, of course.

Why they shot *Forum* in Spain, I'll never know. Someone on that picture must have been sold a fancy tourist bill of goods. Probably they were told about Sunny Spain. They'd forgotten about The Rain in Spain, which that particular year was not confined to the Plain. It also rained on the set of *Forum* about 60 percent of the time.

In the morning, when Jack and Z would get into the car, the driver, having caught on to the main concern of a movie on location (would the sun come out or not), would look up at the sky. If it was cloudy, he'd say, "No *sol*," and Zero would say, "No *sol*, you son of a bitch," and hit him with his hat. After a while the driver learned the whole line, and he'd say, "No *sol*, you son of a bitch," then wait like a straight man to be hit.

On the night before Zero and I were to go to Spain for a little vacation, he called to say he'd like to bring Stanley Prager and a friend of his over for a bite to eat after the show. Why don't men know that you clean out the refrigerator before you go away? What do they imagine happens to the food? So I told Zero we should all go out.

Madeline had stayed late visiting Jack, who was in the hospital with an ulcer attack, and she called to ask if she could come over to say goodbye. The more the merrier, I thought, and when we were finally assembled, we walked over to a nice Jewish-style family restaurant on Broadway called The Tip Toe Inn.

On the way to the restaurant, Zero noticed Madeline's new fur coat. "My wife does not wear coats made of dead animals," he said, in a very high-principled tone. Madeline protested that, in fact, I had a pretty smashing mink coat of my own, and Zero answered, "Those are live minks."

Zero was king at the Tip Toe. His oversize hamburger came on a huge serving platter, and he got the best of everything. We were settled in for a nice evening, with Zero on a special chair (you would have thought it was a throne, the fuss they made about bringing it out), when Stanley's friend told the story of a mutual acquaintance who had left his wife and four children to go off with a young actress. He was saying the new wife was "very nice."

I got furious. "Nice?" I hissed. "Nice? You call a woman who gets a man to leave four children and a wife who has cancer nice? I don't call her nice. I call her a 'bleep.' That's what I call her. A 'bleep.'"

Zero stopped whatever act he was doing and said to me in his booming stern voice, "Kathryn, do you have to be the first woman in America to say 'bleep' in public?" His projection of the X-rated word caused more tray-dropping than my angry whisper.

Suddenly, the side door of the restaurant flew open. The door was not in full view of the rest of the patrons, and it was just as well that it wasn't because in came about ten firemen dressed in black raincoats, boots and helmets, dragging a huge hose and one of them brandishing an ax. Clearly, the kitchen was on fire, and for some reason the restaurant didn't want to alarm or stampede their full house and was quietly warning and controlling the patrons. Zero was still admonishing me with his back to the husky firemen "tiptoing in." Stanley stood up and said to the firemen with the ax, "See here, my good man, don't you know this is a kosher kitchen? You can't use a nonkosher ax in there." Zero was still shouting "bleep" when the firemen departed, and he probably distracted a hundred people from storming the exit. So anytime you're in trouble, yell "bleep" instead of "fire."

Josh reminded me about another argument Zero and I had at The Tip Toe Inn. The four of us were seated in a booth when one of our regular dinner fights broke out. Josh and Toby had made their points and then I started. I must have really hit a tender spot,

★★

because Z turned to me and said, "If you keep this up, you won't get that mink coat you've been nagging about." And I said, "Listen, that mink coat has been in and out of the house so many times, I don't want it anymore."

8

★★

$\mathcal{D}$*uring the* $\mathcal{N}$*ew* $\mathcal{Y}$*ork* $\mathcal{HUAC}$ *hearings,*
Committee Counsel Frank S. Tavenner asked Sarah Cunningham
about her work in a play called *The World of Sholem Aleichem.*
Sarah answered that it was one of the proudest acting experiences
of her life.

In fact, *The World of Sholem Aleichem* would also be
remembered as the forerunner of a musical called *Fiddler on the
Roof.*

The World of Sholem Aleichem, based on the stories of
several Yiddish writers, was written by Arnold Perl. It opened in the
spring of 1953 at the Barbizon Plaza Hotel, which, as you may know,
is not exactly on Broadway. Almost everyone in the show was blacklisted, and the cast included, among others, Morris Carnovsky, Howard Da Silva, Ruby Dee and Jack Gilford. They were paid $125 a
week and were delighted with even that. Herschel Bernardi, Howard
Da Silva's understudy, gave out the programs, and Hesh's wife
Gladys ran the tape that played the musical accompaniment to the
show. Ossie Davis and Bernie Gersten were the stage managers.

The show was a big success, but Madeline says that Howard Da Silva, who also directed, did not get properly appreciative notices for his own wonderful performance. When that began to eat at him, he began eating up the cast, and Jack, the kind of person who eats himself up inside under pressure, developed an ulcer. To this day that ulcer is jokingly called Howard Da Silva.

Later, *The World of Sholem Aleichem* was done on coast-to-coast television on *The Play of the Week*. In this version, which is still revived now and then, Zero, Gertrude Berg, Nancy Walker, Lee Grant and Sam Levene joined Jack and Morris Carnovsky (the only members of the original cast) to present these marvelously moving stories.

In *Sholem Aleichem* Jack created the role of Bontche Schweig, a good man who dies and goes to heaven. Ruby Dee, his "spokes'angel," argues his case before God, telling Him what an exemplary human being this little, unprepossessing person has been on earth. Bontche's reward in heaven is that he can have one wish —anything he wants. He thinks for a long minute and then says: "In that case, if it's true, could I have, please, every day, a hot roll with butter." Naturally, there was not a dry eye in the house, and even now people sitting near him in restaurants sometimes send Jack a hot roll and butter as a tribute to Bontche Schweig.

Sholem Aleichem proved that Jewish stories had an audience, so Arnold Perl wrote another play. This one was called *Tevya and His Daughters*. It starred Mike Kellin and was derived from Sholem Aleichem's stories about a milkman named Tevya. The play ran for some months during 1957 in a recital hall next to Carnegie.

About ten years after *Sholem Aleichem* opened at the Barbizon, Joe Stein sent Zero a script for a musical called *Tevye*. Zero read it and didn't like it. It just didn't get to him. So although we hadn't even heard the score, he sent it back, saying, "No, thanks," and the producers began to try to cast the show without him.

One day Walter Matthau was auditioning when suddenly he stopped what he was reading and said, "You know who you should get to play this part, don't you? Zero!"

And from the darkened auditorium came a voice, "If we could get Zero, do you think you'd be reading for it?"

While all this was happening, Joe Stein got together with Jerry Robbins to rework the script. Again they sent it to Zero, and this time Zero and I thought it looked very good. We went to the offices of the company that published the music for Sheldon Harnick and Jerry Bock, and—just like in those old songwriter movies—they sat at an upright piano and sang the songs for us. And *they* were good. When Harnick and Bock were through, Zero sang them some old Yiddish songs he remembered from his childhood. That's what they were doing when I left them: the two writers at the piano and Zero singing those old Jewish melodies (some of which later found their way into the play, slightly altered for Broadway). Shortly after that, Harnick and Bock came to our house and sang a few more songs they'd written in the meantime, and by then the show looked to us like it was going to be something special.

Fiddler went into rehearsal in July. At first, Hal Prince and the other people involved weren't certain that a Jewish show would be able to sustain itself. They didn't think there were enough Jews to keep the show going. So they tried to make it less authentic, more Broadway, less Jewish. Hal even tried to keep the number of Jews in the cast at a minimum.

Zero was not an observant Jew. He never attended services, our sons were not bar mitzvah and we did not celebrate any of the Jewish holidays. But, of course, Zero was very deeply and profoundly Jewish.

I used to say to him, "Zero, you see Jews in front of your eyes like other people see spots." Once in Switzerland, for example, he bought me a ring in a fancy dignified jewelry store—one of those places with lots of polished glass and blue velvet display cases. The man serving us was dressed impeccably in a morning coat, and he was haughty and polite the way those people always are. Zero asked him if he was Jewish, and the man, politely, said no. But Zero wouldn't take no for an answer. Once he'd decided someone was Jewish, that person was Jewish. During the rest of the transaction, he addressed the man in Yiddish and I translated. When we got outside, Zero said, "That man was Jewish. I know these things." I didn't even try to say, "Zero, you're crazy, he was about as Jewish as I am."

Jews in front of his eyes, and *Fiddler* the chance for him to act as Jewish as he really always felt inside.

I'll never forget Zero's reaction when he first saw the costumes. Orthodox Jewish men wear something called ziziths, undergarments with fringes that hang out below their coats. Well, in the first place, the producers decided the fringes shouldn't show. And then the ziziths were made in the prettiest pastel colors you've ever seen: pink, blue, yellow, pale green.

Zero screamed, "What the hell are you trying to do? We'll be laughed off the stage. The ziziths *have* to be white, and the fringes have got to show!"

Oh, Zero, they said, you don't have to be that exact. But he convinced them—by raging and thundering around—that you *did* have to be that exact.

At one point during rehearsal, Zero entered his house on the *Fiddler* set and kissed the mezuzah, the little scroll Jews nail to the frame of the front door.

"Zero, what are you doing that for?" Jerry Robbins said.

Zero patiently explained that Orthodox Jews always kiss the mezuzah when they enter or leave a house.

Jerry said, "No one knows that. They'll think you're crazy."

Zero argued and argued, but Jerry insisted that kissing the mezuzah would only have meaning to about two people in each audience. So ten minutes later, when Zero walked through that door again, he made the sign of the cross. Jerry got the point and the mezuzah-kissing stayed in the show.

I played the piano at home for Zero and taught him all the songs for *Fiddler*. In fact, I taught him "Rich Man" wrong. It wasn't until after he'd learned it my way that I looked at the score and saw how it should have gone: But my version stayed in the show.

One day Zero came home and said they wanted to cut one of the verses from "Rich Man," the part that goes: "If I were rich I'd have the time of my life/To sit in the Synagogue and pray/And maybe have a seat by the Eastern Wall." Well, they wanted to cut the Eastern Wall. So I, the gentile, said, "They're out of their minds. That's what the whole goddamn play is about. I won't have it. You must leave that line in—that's a very important part of the play." I made such a fuss, they didn't take it out. It seems they needed an Irishwoman to keep the show Jewish.

Zero's contract for the first *Fiddler* called for him to get a minimum against 10 percent of the gross, which came out to about $8,800 a week. That seemed like an enormous amount of money— and still does—yet it was nothing compared to what he would have gotten if he'd had a permanent piece of the show. It's no news that people who put even a little bit of money into *Fiddler* became very rich.

But the initial tryouts didn't promise that anyone would be a rich man. The show opened first in Detroit. It got terrible reviews, when it got reviewed at all—in addition to everything else, there was a newspaper strike. One review that did get in print was written by some automobile executive who doubled as the *Variety* critic in Detroit. He said it was terrible. Another critic came down from Chicago and said the show should have been called *Father Courage*: it was boring, rotten, dull. Out of the few reviews, the only good notices went to Zero.

But the people came anyway. The house was packed from

the first day. On opening night I sat next to a woman who had a friend across the aisle, and at the intermission they had this conversation:

"How do you like it? I think it's very good."

"I do, too. I wonder how the Jews feel about it?"

And as they walked up the aisle together, someone else was saying, "I didn't know all that happened to the Jews."

It was a revelation to those people.

Madeline heard the story that a lady in a phone booth during the intermission said, "Morris, you're really missing something. This show's got everything. There's even a pogrom in the first act."

And that's how word got out in spite of the newspaper strike, in spite of those idiot reviews. Mouth to mouth.

A lot of changes were made in the show before it came to New York. For instance, there was a priest in the first version who later was cut. Before Zero accepted the show, Jack also read for Tevya and they kept giving him the scenes with the priest, unsure that sweet Jack could show great anger. (They should have asked Madeline.) "Do You Love Me" was written during the first week in Detroit, and when the show moved to Washington for another tryout they added "Miracle of Miracles."

During the whole run in Washington, everyone was concentrating on a big socko dance number for the end of the second act. Zero was supposed to dance in it with Maria Karnilova, and every day he was given a different scene to learn as a lead-in to the number. But Jerry somehow couldn't come up with a ballet. Soon they were all exhausted from rehearsing and revising and the tension of not getting that number together. They never made it, and I think it's lucky: the simple scene in the second act—where the mother and daughter, Chava, meet in silhouette behind a scrim at the back of the stage—is much more moving than any big ballet could have been.

The reviews in Washington were great, and the show was completely sold out. But the cast was *worn* out. They'd been rehearsing and on the road for more than two months. One night in the second act Zero was so overtired that the doctor refused to let him go on, and Paul Lipson, his understudy, went on instead. Later, the producers said this was the moment they first knew the play would be a hit—it was a success even without Zero that night.

Zero's *Fiddler* contract ran for one year—September 1964 to August 1965. Howard Rodney, Zero's dresser, remembers that one of the chorus boys came up to him the day before Zero was scheduled to leave and said, "Oh, I feel so guilty. I've just bought a pair of pants for fifty-five dollars."

Howard said, "What do you feel guilty about? You didn't steal the pants, did you?"

"No," answered the boy, "but they cost so much money, and the show is sure to close when Zero leaves." Of course, it didn't close, and although *Fiddler* made Zero a national folk hero, there were a lot of other Tevyas in companies. Not only on Broadway but all over the world—including Japan.

In 1971 Lee Guber wanted Zero to be in a production of *Fiddler* at the Westbury Music Fair on Long Island. He called Sam Cohn, Zero's agent, who turned him down.

The next day Madeline, who sometimes works with Lee as a producer, called me and said, "Kate, I don't know how rich you are, but if Zero can turn down this much money you must be *very* rich."

I discovered that they were offering Zero $30,000 a week for a three-week run.

That night I cagily approached him: "Listen, Sam Cohn has said no, but they want you so much, why don't we just go and see what the theater's like?" Zero replied that he didn't want to do *Fiddler,* he'd done *Fiddler.* Finally, I convinced him it might be a new thing to do it in the round at Westbury, and we drove out to the Island. Zero began to walk around the stage, and when he said, "You know, we could have 'Sunrise, Sunset' up in the aisles," I knew he'd do it.

The show opened in Westbury with no ads. Hal Prince wouldn't let any ads run within thirty miles of New York because *Fiddler* was still on Broadway in its final run and the movie version had just opened with the Israeli actor Topol playing Tevya. In spite of that competition *Fiddler* broke all records and played to standing room audiences every night in Westbury. Jennie Ventriss played Golda and Madeline's sister Thelma Lee played Yente.

In 1975, when Zero was out on a tour of the show, he told me, "Kate, there's really something about me in this role. People love it. Old ladies grab me by the hand. I don't know what it is, but they love me as Tevya." So I suggested that he do a final, farewell tour of *Fiddler,* then give the costume to the Museum of the City of New York and say goodbye to Tevya forever.

I thought he could go to all the cities he'd never played Tevya in. I also thought he could make a lot of money so he wouldn't have to work so hard for the rest of his life.

We went to Sam Cohn with the idea, and Sam said, "A tour like that will have to involve the Shuberts because they own all the theaters." And so we got the Shuberts and the Niederlanders and Roger Stevens, and *Fiddler* went on a six-month tour that broke every record, with full houses in every city.

The last tour of *Fiddler*—this time with Thelma Lee as Golda—played in Los Angeles, Denver, St. Louis, Washington, New Orleans, Detroit, Miami and New York.

Fiddler closed in New York in June 1977. In July we went to London, where Zero taped a segment of the *Muppets* TV show. Then Zero spent the rest of the summer learning his lines for his new play, *The Merchant.* It took him most of our month on Monhegan to get the part down before the show went into rehearsal in New York.

On the first day of rehearsal the actors sit around a table with their books open and, though they've already studied them, actually read their lines through. Zero appeared on that day without the script and went through the entire three-hour play without looking at a page or flubbing a single line. The whole cast applauded. (Many weeks later, an actor he was doing a scene with repeatedly forgot his part and had to ask the prompter to give him the line. Suddenly, Zero was saying to the stage manager: "What's my next line?" Of course, he was only trying to help the other actor relax a bit.)

Zero deeply believed in *Merchant.* He loved the part, and he thought the story was important because it addressed some deep-seated issue of anti-Semitism that the Shakespeare version had perpetuated. He was looking forward to opening in Philadelphia.

The first run-through in Philadelphia lasted three hours and twenty minutes, and after weeks of rehearsal and the general aggravation that accompanies any play in that phase, Zero was very tired. Just before the first Saturday matinée, he was in the dressing room with Howard Rodney. In full make-up, his beard and wig in place, wearing the long robe and skullcap of Shylock, he suddenly turned to Howard and said that he didn't feel well, that his throat felt strange, that he felt dizzy. Howard assumed that it was nerves, the usual pre-curtain tension that can make your throat tighten up. He told Zero to lie down for a while, since they still had ten minutes before the curtain went up. Zero lay down on the couch and Howard sat next to him, holding his hand, putting ice on his head—because he didn't know what else to do. Zero seemed so frightened.

The stage manager decided that a doctor should be called. He came within a few minutes and after examining Zero decided that for safety's sake he should be checked into a hospital. There was one right across from the theater.

The first thing they did, of course, was take a cardiogram. As he was lying there with the electrodes still attached, a doctor in a white coat ran in, waving a piece of paper. He wanted an autograph. The other doctor looked shocked and suggested that first they unplug Zero. And the autograph hunter, looking a little sheepish, said what they all say: "It's not for me. It's for my children."

The cardiogram was perfect, but the doctors thought it would be better to keep Zero in the hospital overnight. He called me to tell me not to worry, but of course I worried and the next day I went to Philadelphia. By the time I got there, they had released him from the hospital. But during the night he again didn't feel well and so was readmitted. Still, all the tests were negative. The diagnosis was a virus called Coxsackie, named after a little town in New Jersey where it was first diagnosed. Howard asked Zero how he could have gotten such a virus, and Zero answered, "Some cocksucker from Coxsackie gave it to me."

In Monhegan I had fallen and hurt my leg, which required a skin graft, so when Zero was told he had a simple virus and needed only a few days' rest in the hospital, he ordered me back to New York to keep the appointment with my own doctor. He'd been furious at me for coming in the first place.

Sam Levene and Howard were the only two people Zero permitted to visit him in the hospital. One day, while Sam was waiting for Zero to come back from some test they were giving him in another part of the building, an intern came by and asked where Mr. Mostel was.

"I don't know," said Sam, "they took him to a hospital."

"This *is* a hospital," said the intern as he ran from the room.

And once, when Zero was again out being tested, the hospital rabbi came in. He asked Sam if he thought Zero could give him elocution lessons.

"You see," he said, "I have this little voice, and when I say,

'The Lord is my Shepherd,' it doesn't come out the way some of my colleagues say it. I want it to sound like 'THE LORD IS MY SHEPHERD,' not 'the lord is my shepherd.' Do you think Mr. Mostel could help me with that?"

Sam told him that he had come to exactly the right person.

Another time, two nice little elderly ladies came to Zero's room to deliver magazines. They had smiles on their faces which said, "We're going to meet the famous Zero Mostel." Instead, however, on the bed sat Sam Levene. The smiles drained away, and Howie was just about to tell them that they were in the presence of another famous actor when one of the ladies turned to Sam and said, "Are you related to Mr. Mostel?"

Sam replied, "I'm his brother."

"I'm so sorry that your brother is in the hospital," the lady said.

"I'm not," said Sam.

She looked at him in horror. "Oh, you mean because he's getting such good care here."

And Sam responded, "I don't care what kind of care he's getting. I can't stand him. Never could stand him."

At that, the ladies dropped their magazines and fled.

They didn't carry what Zero wanted to read anyhow—good art magazines—and Howie was sent out to get them.

On Thursday, September 8, Zero was supposed to be released from the hospital. In the morning Howie brought him the art magazines, special ones he'd gone all over the city to find. Zero was in marvelous spirits. He had phoned Howie earlier and told him to be on call all during the day so that "the minute the doctors sprung him" he could leave. Then he told him he'd just ordered fifteen wonderful, heavy rocks.

Howie said, "Rocks?"

Zero said, "Rocks. Fabulous rocks, so that when you come

to pick up my luggage, you'll have heavy packages to carry. And don't bring shopping bags. Buy some valises for my stuff. Remember, I'm a star!"

Later in the day, he asked Howie to go across the street to Rose's restaurant (one of the best Jewish restaurants in Philadelphia) and order fish—a lot of fish, broiled. And vegetables, chicken broth, pickles, pimientos, delicious rye bread. Rosie, like all restaurateurs, loved to cater to Zero's appetite, even though Zero was famous for restaurant lines like:

"Throw this in the chef's face with my compliments."

Or:

"My lawyers will speak to you in the morning, but don't worry—knowing my lawyers, you'll win and we'll split the profits."

Howie went across the street and Sam stayed with Zero. Of course, Zero didn't approve of the art magazines Howie had brought, so Sam told him, "Listen, tomorrow you'll be out of here, and we'll go and get the right magazines and I'll even get you a copy of *Hustler.*"

At that moment Zero said, "I feel dizzy, call the nurse." And then he collapsed, falling off the bed and hitting his head on the night table.

A little while later, Howie, his hands full of fish and soup in brown paper bags, arrived to find Sam Levene in the hall outside of the room.

Zero had died instantly of a burst aorta.

So *The Merchant* opened in New York without him. His understudy, Joseph Leon, played the part of Shylock. But Howie insisted that Joe wear Zero's yarmulke with his name inside. He wanted Zero to be part of that show.

What was Zero going to do after *Merchant?* John Dexter, the director, had asked him to play Aaron, a non-singing part, in Schoenberg's *Moses and Aaron.*

When Zero told me about it, I said, "Not Schoenberg. There are no tunes in Schoenberg."

And Zero answered, "Dummy, I was a stand-up comic. What other stand-up comic ever had a title role in the Metropolitan Opera?"

He also had told Howie he had an idea for a one-man show called *Parts I Should Have Played.* He was going to have a wonderful time doing all those things in Urdu that he always longed to do. Would have sold out, too, I bet.

During the blacklist, when every day was sure to produce at least one shot in the gut, I had a superstition. If I turned on the radio and the first piece I heard was by Brahms, then it was going to be a good day. It was a minor comfort, but if Brahms was playing, it really held me together. When Zero died, a thought came into my mind and it has stayed there quietly ever since—not bothering anybody, but there.

"No more Brahms," it whispers to me. "There's going to be no more Brahms."

DISCARDED —— W.P.L.